THEN AN

GEN

MARJORIE

Alexander the Great

NAOMI MITCHISON

Illustrated from contemporary sources by

ROSEMARY GRIMBLE

LONGMAN

LONGMAN GROUP LTD
London

*Associated companies, branches and representatives
throughout the world*

First published 1964
Sixth impression 1974

ISBN 0 582 20394 5

ACKNOWLEDGEMENTS

The map on page 24 *is* based on *Cambridge Ancient History* Vol. VI, by permission
of Cambridge University Press.

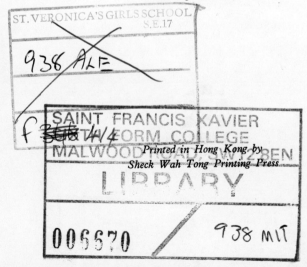
*Printed in Hong Kong by
Sheck Wah Tong Printing Press*

CONTENTS

BOYHOOD OF ALEXANDER   Page 1

THE INVASION OF PERSIA   17

ALEXANDER IN EGYPT   31

THE END OF DARIUS   40

IN SAMARKAND   48

INTO INDIA   54

THE ENDS OF THE WORLD   62

THE GREAT LOVING CUP   72

THE END   82

AFTERWARDS   85

HOW DO WE KNOW?   88

THINGS TO DO   89

GLOSSARY   91

To the reader

Sooner or later everyone with historic or poetic imagination gets excited about Alexander. I in my turn found myself deeply interested in him, above all his idea of human brotherhood called "Homonoia". I know Greece, as well as parts of the furthest country which he reached. I have talked to people in Swat for whom the invasion of Alexander the Two-Horned was something that happened in their immediate past. I have seen the strange wooden warrior figures of the "Red Kaffirs" which, some say, represent Alexander's horsemen. I know Karachi and Gwadur. Never throughout his world will Alexander be forgotten.

Naomi Mitchison

List of plates

facing
page

The young Alexander 4
 (*Mansell*)

The Parthenon high over Athens 4
 (*J. Allan Cash*)

Desert country 5
 (*Barnaby's*)

One of the great rivers of Mesopotamia 5
 (*Courtesy Iraq Petroleum Co., Ltd.*)

Twisting through the Khyber Pass 56
 (*The Press Attaché, The High Commission for Pakistan*)

The north-west frontier of India 56
 (*Royal Geographical Society*)

Statue of Alexander by Lysippos 57
 (*Courtesy Captain Spencer Churchill*)

Through the olive groves to Delphi 57
 (*Stephen Harrison*)

[handwritten: Alexander was born in 356 BC, more than two thousand years ago. His parents were Queen Olympias and King Philip Macedon]

Boyhood of Alexander

In summer of the year 356 B.C., more than two thousand years ago, Queen Olympias and King Philip of Macedon had a baby son. Perhaps King Philip was more excited because his horse had won in the recent Olympic Games than because his wife had a child, but Queen Olympias felt in her heart and always believed that this child, who was to be Alexander III of Macedon, had been fathered by a god. This was not a strange or impossible idea, especially for a princess who was only partly Greek. It all depends on people's ideas about gods and half-gods. And this kind of idea was different in Athens and Macedonia.

For both Alexander's parents were partly, as the pure Greeks would have said, *barbarians*. Macedonia was on the edge of beyond, north of the real Greece, *Hellas* of the *Hellenes*, where people lived in small states cut off from one another by mountain ridges, and invented *democracy*, freedom of thought and

Coin of King Philip with his winning horse

I

speech and equal justice for all citizens. We take these kind of things for granted now, but it was the Greeks who first thought of them and wrote and discussed endlessly about them and taught them to an ever widening circle of the Mediterranean world.

Athens had been the most alive and exciting of the city states, where plays were written so beautiful and some-times so funny that we can still laugh and cry at them. Plays by Aeschylus, Sophocles, and Aristophanes still set modern poets and actors on tiptoe to do their best. Although private citizens did not bother to have grand houses, the houses of the gods and especially of Athene, the Lady of Athens, were spacious and beautiful with marble and statues, pillars and *colonnades*. Here the citizens could meet and argue and talk about politics or justice, foreign affairs, astronomy or poetry or trade, or plain gossip. And it was the same in the other city states: Thebes, main city of Boeotia, Sparta, Achaea, Phocis and the rest. These democracies of the Greek valleys were quite small. Any fair-sized town in Great Britain has more inhabitants than the free citizens of a Greek city state. There were women and slaves as well, but they didn't count. They had no votes, but remember women had no votes in this country fifty years ago.

The city states were always fighting one another. The young men were killed, the corn fields were burned, the olive trees were cut down. Here and there a few people, notably the Athenian Isocrates, had a better idea—for all Hellenes, that is to say all Greeks, to join together in a league which could beat off all outside enemies whom they called barbarians because they said ba ba instead of talking Greek, like civilised people. For there had been war, especially with the great empire of Persia, which

2

Map showing Macedonia and the main Greek states

had only just been defeated, mostly by the Athenians, and at great cost in human lives.

But in the year 357 B.C. the threat was not from Persia but from the young and intelligent King Philip of Macedonia in the north. He had reorganised his army, planning it very carefully and forming a special corps who were called 'The Companions'. These were the proud and brave Macedonian nobles and their sons, who thought of their King as one of themselves, the one they had chosen to be their leader. They had special honours and privileges, but were expected never to fail as soldiers.

3

Most of them were horsemen; there were plenty of horses in Macedonia, and they had more practice than any Greek cavalry. The main Macedonian weapon was a long pike, the *sarissa*, terrifying to men armed only with short lances or swords. This was used by the foot soldiers in the *phalanx*, the heavy-armed, heavy-shielded main body of the army.

At first Philip began interfering in the affairs of Greece as the ally of one or another city state. The constant wars that were going on all the time gave him his opportunity. Alexander was still a little boy living with his mother and her ladies, including his nurse, the noble girl Lanike, in the women's part of the palace at Pella, the capital of Macedonia. He did not see much of his father, who was securing himself by gradual conquest of his neighbours to the south, getting always nearer to the heart of Hellas. And in Athens the statesman and *orator* Demosthenes was rousing the Athenians to the danger they were in. But Athens was a lively democracy, with at least two parties, and there were other orators who were all for Philip, thinking they could get him on to their side.

To begin with Philip acted peaceably; no doubt he hoped for the overlordship of Athens and all the other Greek states in time. There were attempts at settlement, but each of the main states wanted Philip's help against the others. They seem to have been unable to see how this was bound to end. In the year in which Alexander was ten years old, his father, although a Macedonian, was invited to preside over the Pythian Games, a great honour, for these Games were not just athletic events, but also religious rituals, during which a sacred truce was observed by all Greeks.

For three years more, until Alexander was thirteen,

The young Alexander: copy
of a copy, yet it breathes

He saw the Parthenon high over Athens, not then half ruined but towering
in brightness over the Acropolis

Desert country: the kind of thing the armies had to cross

One of the great rivers of Mesopotamia: a water-wheel now as perhaps then, to carry water to the crops

there was a kind of half peace with Athens. Philip probably hated the idea of destroying Athens; he had the kind of love and awe of Athens that many people have had since. And he asked the greatest Athenian of all to come to Pella and be his son's tutor. So when Alexander was about thirteen, Aristotle, the scientist and philosopher, came to the court of King Philip and became in time the greatest influence on the young prince of Macedon. The other influence was his mother, his wild, beautiful mother, who worshipped the gods and goddesses of the forests and vineyards and was most likely herself a priestess. Alexander never gave her less than his heart's love. But Aristotle taught him to observe and think in new ways, taught him above all that the mind must govern the body.

A Prince of Macedon would learn as a child to ride and soon afterwards to shoot with a light bow and use sword and dagger. He would be taken out hunting and learn how to kill. The King's head huntsman riding beside him would point at the track of a wild boar or an antler behind a bush and whisper when he must draw his bow. Probably some of the King's Companions would see to his training for war. But he would not be alone. Other boys of his age would be brought up with him and it seems quite likely that among them were those who would later be his friends and generals. They might be Macedonian nobles' sons, Ptolemy, son of Lagos; Amyntas, Perdiccas, Harpalos, Nearchos who was a Cretan Greek, the son of a great merchant. Perhaps among them was the boy who was to become his dear friend until his death, Hephaestion. The young nobles would not treat the King's son as different from themselves, except for one thing. They were his Companions,

Stag hunt: from mosaic floor at Pella

and as such would die rather than let him come to harm.

If the story of the untameable horse Bucephalus (which means ox-face, because the horse had a white star on his forehead like an ox's) is true, what would they have felt? For the story is that Alexander when only a boy was with his father at a great horse fair—and the Macedonians were good judges of horses—where he noticed the beautiful, savage, nervous beast, and how the thing which really scared him was his own shadow. Alexander asked his father if he could have the horse if he could ride him and his father carelessly said yes. Alexander went over to the horse, taking care that he should face into the sun so that he could not see his shadow, made friends with him and at last mounted and mastered him. Terrifying and glorious for his friends! This was the horse which later he was to ride in battle and after which, many years later, a city was named. We shall never know if this story is true or half true or a pure invention, but it fits in with the character of the young Alexander as we know he must have been, brave and resourceful and masterful, using his imagination intelligently, and not to be kept from anything he wanted.

Probably Aristotle had to be tutor to a whole group of boys, though most of all to the King's son. He would most likely have done a great deal of his teaching out of doors, sitting on stone benches or even walking with them, pointing out the ways of birds and fishes and bees and what could be learnt from them, and encouraging the boys to question him. There were no maps in those days, only a few charts used by ships' captains, giving distances in sailing times; yet he interested Alexander deeply in geography. It was thought in those days that there was a great river, the outer Ocean, running all round the inhabited world, of which the centre—of course—was Greece, perhaps Apollo's temple at Delphi. Nor would there have been many books. Yet there was one which meant a great deal, not only to Alexander and his friends, but to all young Greeks and half-Greeks. This was the poems of Homer, the Iliad (that is, the story of Troy) above all, and then the Odyssey (the adventures of Ulysses). People thought of Homer's poems as in this country some people—almost everyone up to this century—thought of the Bible. It was inspired. It gave the answers, especially to moral problems. Boys must grow up able to quote from it flowingly and easily. Aristotle had a copy of the Iliad written out for Alexander; at that time of course all books were hand-written on *papyrus* or *parchment* and usually rolled on wooden or ivory rollers, so that one unrolled a book instead of turning pages. Alexander's copy of the Iliad had special notes written in it; how I wish we could find it!

But we know that Alexander's special heroes were Achilles and Herakles, both by tradition his ancestors. Achilles was the type of brave and beautiful and generous hero, into whose mouth so much poetry was put, and Herakles was a king who laboured incessantly for the good of others. We know that Alexander kept Aristotle's copy of the Iliad always beside him, night and day.

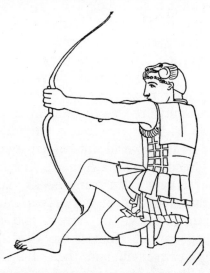

Herakles, traditional ancestor of Alexander: from a statue

Aristotle taught the boys *ethics* and *metaphysics* and something of politics; we know the kind of thing he taught because there are two series of lecture notes which we can still read, Aristotle's 'Ethics' and 'Politics'. But we know less of the kind of science he taught, though there are hints here and there. Aristotle seems to have been, above all, an acute observer—as Darwin was two thousand years

8

later. But he had no microscope nor any of the simplest pieces of apparatus which are used for elementary physics and chemistry today. Yet he roused a scientific interest in Alexander which never left him and he may have done the same for Nearchos, who later commanded Alexander's fleet and was a scientifically-minded explorer

Of course there was plenty in Alexander's young life besides lessons. He certainly went on with hunting and war practice and there were official feasts and probably shows of one sort and another. It is likely that companies of Greek actors, men only, toured round the more important Greek and outlying cities, producing plays which were also in a way religious occasions and often dealt with important moral problems. There were bards and singers who knew thousands of lines of poetry by heart, as people do when there are few books. There were dancers and acrobats and exhibitions of strange animals. If envoys or ambassadors came from a distant city or country, they must be entertained, and the King's son must be to the forefront. There could be gold and silver platters of meat and fish, honey, fruit and nuts, brimming flat cups of wine cooled in mountain snow and constantly refilled. Guests lay comfortably on couches, waited on by pretty girls and boys. All this meant lavish spending, but Macedonia had gold mines. These were worked by slaves, probably in very bad conditions; it would be a terrible punishment for a domestic slave, who was not usually badly treated, to be sent to the mines. But only a few philosophers had begun to think that slavery was wrong; most thought that some people—not themselves— were 'natural slaves' and left it at that. But we may as well remember, especially if we look at some of the magnificent gold coins (called staters) of Philip and

9

Ordinary people of the Hellenic world: pottery figures

Alexander, that, but for the gold, neither of them would have been great conquerors; in fact we would barely have heard of them.

I doubt if anybody, either Aristotle or his father, had the power to stop Alexander from seeing his mother and his young sister; but her relations with his father got worse and worse. There was no law to stop the King of Macedon from marrying as many wives as he chose and Philip went on with this game. Queen Olympias would rage and Alexander took her side.

But much of the time the King was away. The city states were violently for or against him, according to whether or not they thought he would help them in their feuds. Philip did his best to come to a friendly understanding with Athens, but he met too much opposition. Meanwhile he conquered Epirus to the west and this may have been young Alexander's first sight of war. He was thirteen and probably longing to get a taste of the real thing. If he went, the other boys, his Companions, would have gone, all except Harpalos, who was partly crippled and could never be a soldier.

But then it was the turn of the east; Thrace, which had been under Macedonian influence, was now completely conquered and made into part of the Macedonian empire. The mountains of Thrace were cold and wild, but on the sea coast there were Greek trading cities, mostly colonies from the mainland with loyalties towards their mother state, and it was here that war broke out between Philip and the Athenian generals, who had come to try and stop him among the colonies which were in alliance with Athens. It was extremely important to Athens to keep the cities along the Hellespont on her side, because she was not producing enough corn for her population; she had to import it from the Black Sea area. If the corn ships were stopped by an enemy Athens would starve.

In fact war was formally declared when Philip seized two hundred and thirty Athenian merchant ships which were waiting in one of the ports of Propontis for the Athenian warships to take them in convoy. But this fighting ended with something of a defeat for King Philip, who next attacked the Scythians to the north, though much of the booty he got was taken from him in a surprise attack by some wild tribe who came pouring in from the Balkan interior, so that a Macedonian army had to fight its way home.

No doubt Alexander was in some of this fighting, *with his father,* learning as he went along about tactics and siegecraft and the duties and responsibilities of a leader towards his army. He may by now have had his own shield-bearer, Peucestas, who was to stand between him and death in many battles, but during part of the time at least he was ruling Macedonia for his father and learning the business of government.

It seems now that Philip was determined to become complete overlord of Greece and all the city states, even Athens. He marched south, first towards Thebes, where there were two parties, one for him, the other for Athens. Philip's ambassadors were sent to the Theban Assembly; but Athens sent Demosthenes, a wonderful speaker, to argue against them, and the Thebans sided with Athens, as did a number of the smaller states. There was fighting of a minor kind throughout the winter and even when it seemed as though Philip by extremely clever generalship had his armies threatening the combined forces of Athens and Thebes, whose citizen soldiers were no match for the highly trained Macedonians, he tried to settle things peaceably. But it was not to be. The two armies met in August 338, at the Battle of Chaeronea. Alexander, now eighteen years old, commanded on the left with the best of the Macedonian troops. There was fierce fighting from the very first on the left, with Alexander showing his

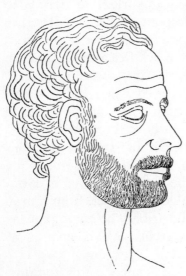

Demosthenes, orator and statesman

father what kind of a fighter and leader he was. It was a complete victory for the Macedonians. Thousands of the Greek citizen soldiers were killed. King Philip celebrated it by an enormous barbaric, boastful feast, refusing even to give up the enemy dead for burial, contrary to all custom at the time. It was only the courage of one of the Athenian prisoners who brought him back to his wise and genuinely civilised self and gave Alexander a lesson in the uses of generosity. It is said, too, that the eighteen-year-old was moved to tears by the sight of the dead Thebans, who had stood their ground to the last until all were killed.

The people of Athens were shocked and terrified at the news of Chaeronea. Yet Philip did not follow it up by complete conquest. The King of the Macedonians forced the Athenians to agree to his terms, but they were fairly merciful. Athens had to become an Ally and never to go against Macedonia. But the young Prince Alexander was sent to the city, bearing the bones of the Athenians who had fallen at Chaeronea and whose bodies had been burned on a huge pyre. In return he was given citizenship of Athens. This must have been his first sight of the city of the philosophers and poets of which he had heard so much. Was it what he expected? Was it the way Aristotle had described it to him? He must have looked at

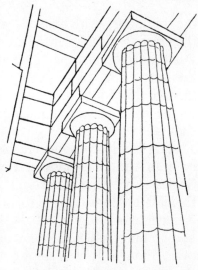

Pillars of the Parthenon, Athens

Steps of the Acropolis, Athens

the buildings with wonder and recognition. That was
the great theatre. That hill crowned with gleaming marble
was the Acropolis, the home of the Goddess. There were
the long walls, going down to the harbour, defence and
menace. No doubt he sacrificed duly, said the right things
to the right people and behaved as a pupil of Aristotle
should.

King Philip consolidated his hold on Greece, pushing
on into the Peloponnese, treating the ancient state of
Sparta also with generosity, though he met little response
there. Now it was time to bring everything together in
one common league, all the Greek states in a political
and military alliance. The day of the little states was
over, though it was a pity that they could not unite
themselves but had to have a conqueror to do it for them,

14

however wise, tactful and far-seeing he might be. The Hellenic League came into being at Corinth late in the year 338, a few months after Chaeronea. Each member was to be independent, but none were to be attacked by another. The seas were to be open for trade by all. There was to be one supreme law court. And finally, the League was to fight for the protection of Hellas from Persian attempts at conquest and for the freeing of the Greek cities of Asia Minor which were under Persian rule.

But King Philip, though he began to prepare for this war of *liberation*, was not to see it fought out. He decided on one marriage too many, to the niece of his general Attalus. At the drunken wedding feast Attalus insulted Queen Olympias, Alexander's mother. Alexander threw his cup in Attalus's face and broke into a furious quarrel

Phillips wedding feast

Scene at a feast: from a vase

15

with his father, who tried to kill him but was too drunk to stand. Alexander and his friends walked out of the wedding feast into exile among the Illyrian tribesmen.

There was a half reconciliation later on and festivities to mark the wedding of Alexander's young sister, Cleopatra. In the middle of it all Philip was murdered by one of his own guards. Some people said the man was in the pay of the Persians, but there were others who thought that this guard was merely the sword in the hand of the insulted and rejected queen.

The Invasion of Persia

The portraits and coins tell us what Alexander was like at nineteen[1]; wavy-haired, fair and cleanshaven, with soft, generous-looking eyes and a way of carrying his head a little to the left. All at once the young King had everything on his hands. The Hellenic League looked as if it might break up, while the tribes to the north were alarmingly active, gathering weapons and singing war songs. He had to be quick. He turned south, cutting steps, still called Alexander's Ladder, up the rock slope of Mount Ossa so as to get over and down into Thessaly, past an army which was holding the mountain pass of Tempe. At that the Greeks, who had breathed a sigh of relief over Philip's murder, began to realise that Philip's son was as much to be feared as Philip had been. He was hastily elected to the Presidency of the Hellenic Council.

Then it was time for his other enemies. What had he on his side? Courage and youth and as good an education as was possible. Devoted friends. Two of the best of his father's generals Antipater and also Parmenion, who had been sent into Asia Minor with an exploratory force, had sided for him, and so almost at once did the army, that is to say the citizens in arms of Macedonia, who considered themselves free to choose whom they would to lead them. Attalus, who had shown his enmity at the wedding feast, was executed. Alexander had his mother,

[1] See plate facing page 4

17

Celtic bronze jug, probably for wine

but though he was devoted to her he did not want interference in the difficult business of reconciliation and the future government of Macedonia. She went back to Epirus, to her own rites and dreams.

Alexander was barely twenty when he led his army east and north and got a hard victory over the Triballi, the first of the menacing tribes, and chased them to the Danube. There again he took quick and decisive action, got more than five thousand men across the Danube in ships or dugout canoes, and scattered the Triballi and their neighbours the Getae, who surrendered. This also brought him *envoys* from the Celts of the upper Danube, enemies of the Triballi, who allied themselves to him with an oath which said: 'We will keep faith unless the sky fall and crush us or the earth open and swallow us or the sea rise and overwhelm us.'

But meanwhile other enemies from Illyria to the west had invaded Macedonia. Alexander had to march quickly, with danger to his flank from the north. But again he defeated his enemies, only to hear that the rumour had been put about Greece that he was dead, the League had broken up, and the anti-Macedonian Theban exiles were back in Thebes. Again Alexander called on his unrested armies for another of those rapid marches which were going to be the keynote of his generalship later. And long before he could have been expected he was under the walls of Thebes, having collected on the way bands of soldiers from the other Greek states that he had marched through. He hoped Thebes would submit, but they were determined to fight. He took the city by storm, burned and pulled down all the buildings except the temples and the house that once belonged to the poet Pindar. For he understood that poetry is really important—more important than war. Many of the Thebans were sold as slaves, although some people felt one ought not to enslave fellow Greeks and it may well have troubled a pupil of Aristotle. But at least the punishment stopped any other Greek states from opposing Alexander. Athens submitted and his terms were generous.

So now, with all settled, the time was come for Persia. Why was he determined on the conquest of Persia? Partly because he had been brought up to think it was bound to happen and partly no doubt through the influence of Aristotle and Isocrates and other Greeks who were bound to think of Persia as the enemy who had committed a great wrong on Hellas, which must one day be avenged. Perhaps Alexander felt that if he conquered the great King of Persia he would become the real head of the Greek world. He would be the *liberator* of the cities of Asia Minor. For along the coast of Asia Minor there were rich Greek trading cities, called the Ionian cities, which had been forced to submit to Persia. If he freed them, Greeks everywhere would look on him with love and gratitude; it would wipe out any wrongs he or his father might have done. And were not the Persians, although rich and highly civilised, mere 'barbarians'? He would go ahead.

Alexander was twenty-one when he crossed the Hellespont as Commander-in-Chief of the Macedonian army and the League of Corinth, with three thousand foot soldiers and over five thousand horse. Antipater was left with a much smaller army to look after things at home. There were about the same numbers of Greek and Macedonian infantry, but the best of the cavalry were the Macedonian 'Companions' who were always the first into battle, usually led by Alexander himself.

By now the young men whom Aristotle had taught with Alexander were themselves part of the army, commanding in the phalanx or the Companions, or on the staff, constant friends and advisers. His greatest friend, Hephaestion, on whom he seems to have tried out most of his ideas, was always with him. The army had a well organised siege and baggage train; the chief engineer was Diades, full of ideas about portable *siege towers* and wheeled *rams*. There were surveyors, sappers and well-sinkers. Careful records were kept which could be used by all future geographers. Supplies for men and horses were collected in conquered countrysides, checked and distributed.

But there was more to it than this. Alexander's army had a complete secretarial department, under Eumenes of Cardia, who wrote a daily official record on which much of our knowledge is based. There were philosophers and historians; Aristotle had gone back to Athens, but sent his nephew, Callisthenes of Olynthus, to be with Alexander in his place. But unhappily Callisthenes was a much smaller-minded man than his uncle. There were architects, including the man who later on was to lay out Alexandria in the Egyptian delta, and there were botanists and geographers and observers of all kinds, intent on keeping records, and collecting information and speci-mens, some of which went back to Aristotle. As the expedition went on into Persia and further yet, some

20

would go home but others would take their place. Besides the scientists there were professional poets, with praises for sale, or perhaps attracted like bees to flowers by the glory that was going on. All this keeping of records was very much under Alexander's own eye and so was the training of the royal pages, the boys who were to be the future officers, whose duty it was to watch before Alexander's tent.

Apart from Eumenes' record it is to Ptolemy, son of Lagos, that we owe much of this information; he wrote a history of Alexander's wars, which is more accurate than anything which has survived from the professional historians and literary men. He was himself one of the inner council. Probably Alexander knew he was writing it, perhaps saw it sometimes. He must have felt from the beginning that he was making history.

All this was fine, but the money was running low. Even the Macedonian gold mines could not keep up with the tremendous new expenses. It was essential to capture some of the enormous treasure which belonged to the great King of the Persians and his nobles. How much was that on Alexander's mind when he started on the expedition? And if he did consider it, does that make him a robber? Certainly that was not how people in his own times ever thought of him.

King Darius seems not to have taken Alexander seriously at first. He actually had a lot of well-paid Greek soldiers fighting for him and these *mercenaries* had defeated Parmenion's exploratory force, but had not bothered to drive them back from their bridgeheads on the Hellespont. Even when Alexander's forces began to cross, Darius was slow to act. Although he had good and devoted generals, he was not a great commander-in-chief

21

himself. Perhaps he supposed that the great landowners with their own little private armies, aided by the Greek mercenaries, could deal with these Macedonians. He behaved somewhat as the nineteenth century Chinese Emperors did in face of their invaders. It was Parmenion who superintended the crossing of the Hellespont, while Alexander came by ship to Ilium and sacrificed at the ancient temple of Athene. He had taken on for a time the character, the very look, of his ancestor Achilles. He felt it was right for him, as the new Achilles, to take away with him from Ilium the sacred shield which was to go with him everywhere. At the same time he declared Ilium free. No longer should the famous Homeric city pay *tribute* to Persia!

By now the *satraps*, the Persian governors of the

Arming for battle—but the shield will have to be mended: from a vase

22

provinces, had got their forces together, backed by the landowners and some of the Greek mercenaries, many of whom were in garrisons along the coast, forcing the merchant cities into loyalty to Persia. They had good cavalry and archers, but their infantry were mostly *serfs* or undisciplined hill tribesmen from the interior. The Persians decided to stand at the river Granicus and, if possible, kill Alexander, whom they thought rightly was the key to the whole expedition. Without him the Macedonian invaders would go back.

They nearly did succeed in killing Alexander when he led the cavalry charge across the river, gallant and splendid, with white wings on his helmet and the wonderful horse Bucephalus under him. It was his gallant friend Cleitus the black-haired who saved him. But at last victory went to the Macedonians. The Persians broke and the Greek mercenaries were all either killed or sent back in chains as slave labour in Macedonia, perhaps to the mines. Alexander sent three hundred Persian trophies back to Athens with a dedication from 'Alexander and the Greeks, except the Spartans.'

Then he turned southward into Ionia to bring the Greek merchant cities over onto his side. The Persians had held the towns through Greek rulers who were on their side, no doubt always well supported by Persian money. Alexander, on the contrary, supported government by the people, partly no doubt because Aristotle had taught him that this was the best kind of government and he felt himself, like Herakles, to be doing a noble and liberating work for mankind. He had to fight at Miletus, taking the Persian garrisoned citadel by assault. There was still a strong Persian fleet, but Alexander dismissed almost all his own, taking the risk that the

23

Map of Alexander's route through Asia Minor and south to Egypt

Persians might try and cut his communications; he had no money to go on paying sailors. And again half the Persian fleet was manned by the poorer citizens from the Ionian coastal cities; now that Alexander had proclaimed democracy everywhere, it was worth while for them to go home. They were not going to fight against a man who had freed them from *oligarchies* and tyrants.

24

Next Alexander marched into Caria, where the widowed queen, who had been dispossessed by the Persians and her brother, formally adopted Alexander as her son. He was held up at Halicarnassus, but finally took the town and restored Queen Ada to her possessions. He went on south and east, but now it was winter and he decided to send home all the newly married men in his army on long leave, while he himself with the older men attacked the hill tribes, who had to come down into the valleys in

King Mausolus of Halicarnassus: Greek drapery, barbarian hair

winter. Everywhere he was victorious. His friends were made into governors or satraps and the land taxes, which had been going to the Great King, went instead to pay the Macedonian soldiers. The Persians tried to assassinate him, but he was surrounded by loyalty and enthusiasm. He had his luck, too. Where the steep and savage cliffs of Mount Climax come down to the sea nobody can get round them when the prevailing south wind drives up the water. But the wind changed for Alexander and he marched his men round by the beach, not more than knee deep.

Now he turned north, conquering his way up through Phrygia. At Gordium they showed him the ancient chariot of Gordias, founder of the monarchy, with the yoke lashed to the pole in a complex knot of dogwood *withies*.

The story was that the man who untied the knot would rule Asia. It was not like Alexander to have cut the knot with his sword, but this is the story that was told.

Behind him the Persians were to some extent undoing his work in Ionia but not enough to endanger him. At Ancyra he received formal submission from independent Paphlagonia in the north of Asia Minor, but he never intended to invade the country. What he wanted was to meet and defeat Darius, the Great King himself. One wonders what the Paphlagonian envoys looked like, and whether any of them talked Greek, and what they thought of Alexander. Probably some of them were Greek-speaking, but they would have worn rather odd and barbarian clothes, trousers and heavy *frieze* or fur cloaks, and no doubt plenty of gold chains and bracelets. Alexander would probably have been in armour, beardless and smiling, his friends, young as himself, round him in the draughty linen tent, heated perhaps by a couple of braziers, with little sign of luxury. No singing girls or feasting tables or deep couches such as people associated with conquerors, but all soldierly and simple.

Now again Alexander marched south towards a narrow hill pass, the 'Cilician Gates'. This was supposed to be *impregnable*, and would have been if the garrison had not been taken by surprise, due to one of those incredibly rapid marches of picked troops, led by Alexander himself. He took the gates without losing a man, galloped down into Tarsus with his cavalry, saving the city from being burned by the Persians in a 'scorched earth' policy, but then fell ill in the warm plains. Here a letter came to him from General Parmenion, telling him that his physician friend, Philip of Acamania, had been bribed by Darius to poison him. Alexander, who still loved and trusted his friends as they did him, showed the letter to Philip while he drank the medicine which Philip had given him. Philip read it, shrugged his shoulders and remarked to Alexander, that he would get well if he followed his advice. Alexander did get well!

Now after his recovery Alexander was again campaigning, making sure of the passes out of Cilicia and receiving the submission of the cities. Then he heard that the Great King with his army was in Syria, left his sick and wounded in Issus, and went into Syria towards what he thought would be a great battle. But meanwhile Darius had decided to come and hunt him out of Cilicia and while Alexander was crossing by one pass, the Great King and his armies came over another, marched down onto Issus, killed Alexander's sick and wounded, and realised that they had cut Alexander's communications and could force him to fight facing his own base. Even if they could not completely defeat the invader, it would be as good as a victory to the Persians to hold him cut off.

It is difficult to know how large an army Darius had. There must have been plenty of guesswork and afterwards it was certainly one of the duties and pleasures of the literary men and poets to make out that Alexander had defeated a vast host of Persians. It looks as though the Persian army was rather larger than Alexander's, though not as good. There were perhaps twelve thousand Greek mercenaries in Darius' army, mostly in the centre; if they could hold, Alexander would be cut off. Darius himself and his guard were behind the Greeks in the centre. The Persian position was a good one on the banks of the river Pinarus, their right flank going down to the sea, their left reaching up to the hills. They must have known in Cilicia, and the cities or families who had welcomed

27

Alexander must have been terrified of what would happen to them if the Great King either won the battle outright or held Alexander off.

At first Alexander could not believe that it had happened: that the Persians had cut his communications. He sent a ship to report and the army must have heard what had happened to the sick and wounded, their fellow soldiers and friends. Alexander went in to attack in what he knew must be the crucial battle, with some twenty to twenty-four thousand infantry and five thousand cavalry. He was now twenty-three. He had marched hard and halted to rest his men just out of bowshot.

The first thing he did was to drive the Persian left up the hill and out of action; they were light armed infantry, unable to stand up to his well-trained *javelin* men, but they could have got badly in the way of his charge if they had been left. This done, the Macedonian line started moving. Once within bowshot Alexander led the cavalry charge all out, knowing he must get through. The Persian archers and the troops behind them turned and ran and Darius himself ordered his chariot to be turned

Battle scene: from a low-relief carving

and fled himself, deserting his army which went on fighting. His guard stood and on his right the cavalry under Nabazarnes had charged across the river against Parmenion's cavalry, driving them back. The heavy armed phalanx had lost its order in crossing the river against the Greek mercenaries and there was bitter fighting there. In fact Issus might have been a drawn battle, but that when the Persian army heard that the Great King had fled it went into a fairly orderly retreat. Alexander was wounded and night fell before much damage could be done to the Persians. But the main body of Greek mercenaries on the Persian side were fed up; they marched down to the coast and sailed for Egypt. Here some of them were killed trying to conquer the country, but the rest went back to the mainland and in the end took service with Sparta.

Here for the first time the Macedonians saw what royal Persian luxury really was; the king's chariot and bow were captured, and so was his tent, which one may imagine as a fairytale dome of gold and embroidery and precious stones, sweetly scented with *attar* of roses or jasmine, or smouldering *myrrh*. 'This, I believe, is being a king' said the young Alexander, sitting down at Darius's table to be served with Darius's royal wine and food. But while he and his friends were eating they heard women wailing. These were Darius's mother, wife and two little daughters, who had been taken prisoner and were weeping for the king's death. He sent one of his friends to tell them that Darius had not been killed and that they were safe; they would be treated in the manner due to their rank. He would never allow himself to see or think of Darius's beautiful young wife but he was kind to the mother and in return it seems she became fond of him in a motherly way, like the other queen, Ada. But the praise he had from historians for his good treatment of the women, only shows what a conqueror might have been expected to do.

Golden object from the Oxus treasure

Alexander in Egypt

At this stage Alexander had only half conquered the western end of Persia; his own governors or satraps had an uncertain hold. But he was beginning to get some money into his treasury. Outside the Ionian cities Asia Minor had all been King's land, paying taxes to the Great King through the landowners and satraps, both of whom probably made their own profit. Alexander's system of direct tax collection might be good for the peasants and small farmers but the Persian landowners who had to pay taxes would be less pleased.

In the old days the Ionian Greek cities had to pay tribute money to the Great King. Alexander abolished this and the cities eagerly became his free allies. But he stopped the democrats taking their revenge on their old tyrants and oppressors. He refused to let people inform against those who had sided with Persia, and tried very earnestly *to reconcile* the peoples and parties of the Greek cities. It looks as though he were often personally involved in all this, using all his powers of persuasion. Here, I think, we see Aristotle's pupil again.

He did not even insist on any kind of grand title for himself. In fact, he really and genuinely wanted the Greek cities to be free. As for the native Persian towns, they had no traditions of self-government, no constitutions such as the Greek cities had, and even Alexander could not immediately invent ways in which they could govern themselves.

What was he thinking about as the wound he had got at the battle of Issus skinned over? He had to make a choice now. Was he to be content with the control of Asia Minor and the money he was getting in land taxes and the friendship and alliance of the Greek cities? If so, he must be prepared at any time to fight a defensive war, for the surest thing was that the so-called Great King, Darius, would try to get back this valuable part of his empire. The alternative—and it must have made him blink—was to conquer the whole Persian empire! And perhaps beyond. One can imagine him talking it over with the Guard, his own chosen Companions, and the Council, perhaps with philosophers like Callisthenes, certainly with his friend Hephaestion. The older men would have been doubtful, but some at least of the young ones would have found it all as exciting as space travel is nowadays.

Alexander weighed it up sensibly, but his temperament told him to go ahead. Nor did he have a wife or child back in Macedonia to whom his thoughts could turn. He could write to his mother; perhaps he felt that if and when he came back she was the one permanent person who would always be there. He knew that both Phoenicia and Egypt would welcome the chance to free themselves from the Persians. That meant for a start the destruction of the Persian fleet. He went south down the coast towards Phoenicia and was generally welcome.

Meanwhile Parmenion had gone off across the mountains into Syria and taken Damascus without much fighting. It was full of fantastic booty, including Darius's baggage and war chests. There was no more need now for Alexander to worry about paying his troops! No doubt

32

there was jewellery and armour and gold plate there of such value and such superb workmanship as had never been seen in Macedonia. This was royalty; this was the real thing!

Parmenion also captured the families of many Persians as well as some Greek envoys to Darius. Alexander had several officers among his council who spoke Persian

Golden animal from the Oxus treasure

and could be very useful. Soon he had a letter from Darius asking him, as one king to another, to release his family, and offering him friendship and alliance. This was a chance for Alexander to write a letter putting himself forward as the avenger of Hellas. He said that all this had come about because long ago King Xerxes of Persia had invaded Greece, and, since the Gods remember endlessly, no wrong is ever forgotten. There was much else. He accused Persia of procuring the assassination of his father, King Philip, and attempting to break up the Hellenic League. Finally he said that he—Alexander—was already King of Asia. If Darius wanted anything he must write in humble terms. This claim was only put in to make Darius fight, which he was bound to do. Then Alexander would feel himself thoroughly in the right and at home.

Now the Macedonians were getting into the heart of the trading and shipping area of Phoenicia. Alexander was welcomed at Sidon, but with less certainty at Tyre, the crowded island city, full of factories and secret processes, run ruthlessly by slave labour. As a test Alexander asked to be allowed onto the island to sacrifice to Melkart, the god whom we know as Moloch, and whose *rites* were much disapproved of by the Hebrews, but who was *equated* by the Greeks to a form of Herakles —Alexander's ancestor. The Tyrian envoys said they would not have any strangers in their city (though he was welcome to sacrifice to his ancestor on the mainland).

That warned Alexander that he was not going to get control of Tyre without a siege. He began building a *mole* out from the mainland, easy enough in shallow water, very difficult in deep water, harassed by arrows from the walls and attacked by Tyrian warships. He got two siege towers out to the end of the mole, but the besieged garrison of Tyre answered with a fireship which was grounded on the mole and dropped baskets of flaming material—something perhaps which neither Greeks nor Macedonians knew—onto the towers. The mole was torn down and Tyre rejoiced. But Alexander started building a new and broader one.

Yet he could see that he must have ships. He sent to Sidon and collected a large fleet, partly from the other Phoenician cities, who looked on Tyre as their most dangerous rival, partly from Rhodes and Cyprus and other Greek city states. He began to build new siege machines, rams, towers, catapults, the lot, but decided himself to lead the most important part of the battle, this time from the sea. The Tyrian fleet stayed in harbour, knowing they were no match for Alexander's mixed armada, but as his ships got near the walls the besieged started firing at them. Rocks had been dropped into the sea to wreck any ship sailing too close in. When merchant vessels were brought up to sweep for the rocks, Tyrian warships attacked

34

them and cut their anchor cables, or perhaps the cables attached to grabs; when Alexander protected them with his own warships, divers—as brave as frogmen though less well equipped—cut the cables. At last by using chains instead of ropes the sweepers could get the rocks out. There was more sea fighting and then a combined assault by land and sea. Two ships got bridges out to a *breach* in the city wall. Alexander was one of the first to cross. Then the Tyrian defence broke, after a siege lasting seven months.

It was a horrible massacre, eight thousand fighting men killed, many others, with women and children, sold as slaves. Only a few found safety in the temple of Melkart. It was, in the ancient world, the undoubted right of a conqueror to sell his captives, but Alexander only did this when there was some special reason for his anger. That is something we must remember in his favour. But Tyre for the moment was finished, and Sidon took the lead in Phoenicia.

Meanwhile there was another letter from Darius, this time offering to give up to Alexander the whole of his empire west of the Euphrates as well as a ransom of ten thousand gold talents for his family, and the hand of his daughter in marriage. It is said that when Alexander told his generals of the offer, Parmenion said were he Alexander he would accept; Alexander answered that he too would accept, were he Parmenion, which cannot have endeared him to Parmenion and the older generation of Macedonians. In any case he refused to negotiate with Darius.

He did not even wait to take Syria. He left Parmenion to deal with Damascus and the country round about and himself hurried south towards Egypt. He was wounded again in the battle before Gaza, but got to Egypt in late

November. The people of Egypt recognised him at once as their liberator and avenger and the Persian satrap wisely surrendered. Now Alexander went up the river Nile to Memphis. I hope he gave himself time to go by boat, recovering from his wound, unintently watching the patterns of men or birds fishing, seeing the water laboriously taken up for *irrigation*, the rising and dipping of the poles, seeing the lines of laden donkeys or women, the unending business of the Egyptian peasants, working many of them on temple lands, for the priesthood, who were also unendingly busy, but on matters connected with death and the ways to avoid the death of the other part of man, not the body, but the various kinds of soul. The peasants, doubtless, would perish, but not those who had learned the secrets of the priesthood, who could pass the gate of the serpents and answer the judge of the dead. Nobles were priests and priests were nobles. Pharaoh, the ruler of upper and lower Egypt, was also in close relation to the Gods. At Memphis Alexander sacrificed to Apis, no doubt satisfactorily to the priesthood and at suitable cost. He was duly recognised as Pharaoh reborn.

He came down the river again under the velvety sky and stars clearer and brighter than ever they were at home. He discoursed with his friends, perhaps with his philosophers and poets. But not with the lovely girls who would no doubt be eagerly provided and who would dance, perhaps better than most of them nowadays, for him alone. This he refused, believing in the mastery of the body, just as he had refused even to see Darius's beautiful wife who could have been his by the law of conquest.

Who was with him in the barge coming down the Nile,

Apis, the Egyptian bull-god

with the continuous trickle of the drops falling from the oar blades and the light bow wave? Almost certainly Hephaestion, his greatest friend, the one man perhaps who really followed the workings of his mind. Perhaps Philotas, son of General Parmenion, or Cleitus, who had saved his life at the battle of Granicus, whose sister Lanike had been his nurse when he was a child. Perhaps Ptolemy, son of Lagos, never foreseeing that one day he would be ruler of Egypt and his descendants after him, to the last and greatest of them, Cleopatra, who ended the dynasty in a kind of glory he would not have understood. Callisthenes the philosopher, might have been there; perhaps he was thinking that now Alexander had the treasures of Persia to spend he might rebuild Olynthos, Callisthenes' home town, which had been destroyed by King Philip sixteen years before. In those days people were in some ways more used to the uncertainties of human life than we are. But most of them had fewer possessions. The temples of a city were seldom destroyed by the worst conqueror, or only by accident. It took cannon and gunpowder to destroy the Parthenon at Athens many centuries later. Perhaps, thought Callisthenes, if I speak well of Alexander, give him public praise, his mind will turn to my city.

But Alexander was intent first of all on founding another city on the Nile *delta*; it would replace ruined Tyre as a great Mediterranean port. So he planned the great city of Alexandria though perhaps already he was thinking beyond the Mediterranean towards other oceans. Alexandria might stand between two worlds.

And now it was time for him to visit the *oracle* of Ammon. This, with Delphi and Dodona, were the great oracles of the Greek world. Ammon had been adopted into the Hellenic family of gods. Alexander had probably already visited Delphi. Now he must consult another messenger of the future. But he did not take either of the regular pilgrim routes. Instead he went along the coast to Cyrene, in disguise, with only a few friends, and then struck inland. The story is that he was guided through the desert to the oasis of Siwa, where the shrine of the oracle was, by birds or serpents. In any case he went alone into the shrine and was greeted by the priest, who doubtless had been warned of his coming, as Pharaoh, son of Ammon. In the terms of the ritual, Alexander, like other Pharaohs, was given 'dominion over the whole world'. What else the oracle told him he kept to himself, unless, perhaps, he wrote about it to his mother.

He stayed all that winter in Egypt, very much impressed not only with the great *fertility* of the country, but with its possible strength should it decide to revolt. He arranged the government of Egypt in a reasonable way, not as a tyrant would. He wanted to have all the countries which had surrendered to him not as conquered lands, but as friends. Perhaps already he was sometimes imagining the future in terms of a general brotherhood of all mankind and looking for the peace and wisdom which must be found somewhere at the back of all this fighting. He was broadening out Aristotle's ideas into something wider than a city state, wider than Hellas, wider than the Mediterranean world.

Golden bracelet, Persian: from the Oxus treasure

The End of Darius

Darius meanwhile was desperate to fight and defeat Alexander, who had beaten his unconquerable army and mortally insulted him. He wanted a pitched battle and he wanted to drive his chariot over the bleeding body of his hated enemy. He had good and devoted generals, but not one of them was a military genius. Alexander was. However they thought up one new, or rather *refurbished* weapon, the *scythed chariot*. These were not easy to drive or manoeuvre. If you were not skilful you were likely to cut off the legs of the next man's chariot horses. But it might work against the Greeks.

Alexander was now back in Phoenicia. He joined Parmenion and advanced across Syria; he crossed the Euphrates and Tigris, passing the ruins of Nineveh and many another ruin of earlier civilisation.[1] He may well have noticed the broken down irrigation and drainage canals and the rich lands of Mesopotamia which had once been full of crops and flourishing villages, but were now in many places turning into stinking swamps. In the course of a few battles the irrigation system, which had been built up by generations of Babylonian farmers and governors had been smashed up. The army doctors may have noticed an increase in fevers, which often killed their patients; they did not connect them with mosquitoes and swamps.

[1] For Alexander's route from this point see endpaper.

A great lady of a Syrian city: a portrait statue

The Persians had taken up battle position on a flat plain near the village of Gaugamela. Here the scythed chariots would have every chance of doing their worst. Darius himself was in the centre. He had cavalry and archers from all ends of his empire, from Parthia, Bactria and far Sogdiana at the back of the Himalayas, as well as westerners, including still a few Greek mercenaries. He also had fifteen elephants from Arachosia, who once perhaps had trampled in the mud of the river Indus. But perhaps they were not as useful as they might have been, since they probably frightened not only the horses of

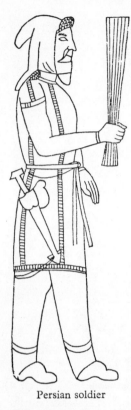
Persian soldier

their enemies but also their own. However, it is clear that Darius had a large army, larger than the one Alexander had faced on the Issus, with the best of the Persian generals in command, especially Mazaeus on the right.

It seemed to Alexander fairly certain that they would try and *outflank* him and probably succeed, but if his army was prepared that would not matter. So he drew up his own men in three sides of a square, ready to meet any outflanking movement. Even if his army was surrounded, the second line behind the phalanx had orders to complete the square.

Alexander saw to it that his whole army had a good dinner and sleep. His own armour was ready for him: helmet of iron polished as bright as silver, his sword and jewelled sword belt. Then, knowing that he had thought out all possible contingencies, he went to sleep himself and slept well. This ability to sleep deeply and quickly may have been what brought Alexander through some of his incredibly tough adventures, marches, climbs, battles, endless planning and organisation, which would have exhausted anyone who was not able to relax completely when the moment came. Now it was the 1st of October, 331, and he was twenty-five.

When the scythed chariots charged, the javelin men were ready, spearing horses and riders, so that all were

42

thrown into confusion; ranks were opened to let any surviving chariots drive helplessly through and be finished off. Along the rest of the line there was attack and counter attack, but Alexander was keeping back the Companions until he saw a gap in the Persian line. Then at the head of the Companions he charged the gap. The Persian line broke. As before, Darius turned and fled.

All was not well on Alexander's left, where Parmenion's part of the line broke under Persian pressure. Persian cavalry under Mazaeus rode right through the phalanx cutting it in two. Things looked bad and Parmenion sent a messenger to Alexander for help. Alexander turned and rode back at the head of the Companions. There was heavy fighting and sixty of them were killed, but now news had got through to the Persians that their Great King had again deserted them. They turned and fled, some in their units, still undefeated and angry, others in disorder. Alexander pursued them till nightfall, rested a few hours, mounted again and never stopped till he reached Arbela, sixty-two miles away.

Mazaeus had taken his men as far as Babylon; he did not mean to defend the city, whose great walls had long been destroyed, and he was sick of serving a king who ran away. He came out to meet Alexander, who received him with honour as a brave man and made him satrap of Babylon. This may have shocked some of the Macedonians but it was a wise move. Meanwhile he restored to the Babylonians their native customs which they had lost under Xerxes and started to rebuild E-sagilla, the temple of the god Marduk which Xerxes had destroyed. Then he rode east again, leaving Darius's womenfolk at Susa.

Now he was pressing on into the heart of the Persian empire; he came to the pass called the Persian Gates, was

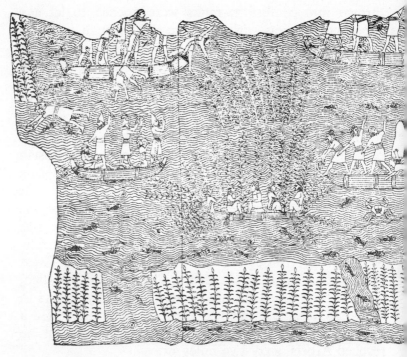

beaten back, but with a few hundred men and three days'
food climbed over the snow-covered range and took the
defenders in the rear. That was the kind of risk that it
kindled his heart to take. Now he rode on, the great
shoulders of Bucephalus moving steadily under his
knees, making for the palaces of Persepolis and the
treasure he knew was there, heaven high on the mountain
terraces.

It was there, out of this world! More gold in bars and
coin than in the whole of the western cities, besides
jewels and plate, Indian silks and Tyrian dyes! He burned
Xerxes' palace to show the Greeks that the dead of
Thermopylae and Marathon were avenged, and to show

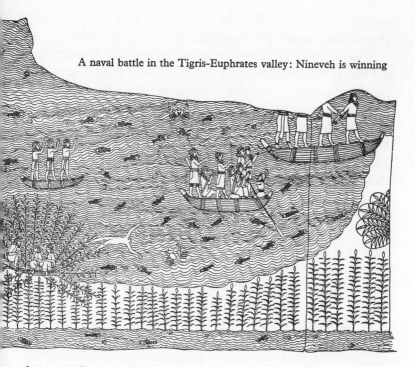

A naval battle in the Tigris-Euphrates valley: Nineveh is winning

the east that the Persian empire was ended. In spring he went on to Ecbatana, skirting the great salt desert, and there waited for a little. Between battles and the planning and organisation, both of conquest and of the administration of the conquered places, as well as the handling of the new people he must deal with so that they would be as friendly as possible, what Alexander most liked was hunting. This had all the skill and excitement of battle—and some of the risk. In Persia he hunted lions, spearing them from horseback, and had some narrow escapes. He stayed on for a time in Ecbatana, excited, perhaps, by the strangeness of the palace, wondering what would happen next. For Darius could never bring together another army or the old loyalty. Persia as a military power was as good as finished.

Now he would have to organise this vast empire, into whose possession he had tumbled, for peace, and this might be more difficult than war. And first he must forget the old story that non-Greeks were natural slaves. When he made Mazaeus satrap he had given the lie to that, and now he appointed two more Persian satraps. But he must persuade Greeks and Macedonians that this was the new way of thinking and feeling and acting Perhaps he talked it over with Hephaestion. Perhaps he used the Greek word 'homonoia', equal friendship, but would the older generals understand what he was after? For that matter would the young ones?

Yet he loved them, his Macedonians. Harpalos had done something earlier on, some dishonesty perhaps, which had made Alexander angry. But Alexander recalled and forgave him with his whole heart and put him in charge of all the financial arrangements and communications. For a time it worked, but not, unhappily, for long; Harpalos's greed was too much for him. But generally Alexander could feel free among his Macedonian friends; he need not be always keeping up his position; they could get drunk together; he could lose his temper with them but it was all right the next day. Many of them were kings' sons too. Most of them loved him.

Meanwhile Darius and a few of his followers had crossed over into eastern Iran, a quite other part of the empire, to which Issus and Gaugamela were not very real. He began to try and collect troops. Alexander followed at an exhausting and almost incredible speed. As they made their camp one evening Mazaeus's son rode in to say that three of the chief men, including his kinsman Bessus, had deposed Darius, the Great King, and were holding him prisoner.

In yet greater haste Alexander set off for Bessus's camp. He marched thirty-six hours with only one break and found Bessus gone; he could have only a few remnants of the great Persian army with him now. Alexander marched another sixteen hours to a village, where Bessus had halted with his prisoner the day before, then heard of a short cut across the desert. With only five hundred mounted men, he led the way; when all were thirsty he would not drink himself. They rode fifty miles until they saw the dust cloud—the men they were after—who saw them. Two of them stabbed Darius and left him lying in the desert while they galloped away. The first Macedonian who got to the place gave Darius a cup of water; he was dead before Alexander saw him. A living Darius would have been enormously embarrassing. Dead, he could be covered honourably with a purple cloak and sent to be buried at Persepolis.

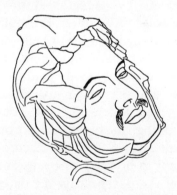

Sculptured head of a dying Persian

In Samarkand

The next few months were spent tidying up, securing the loose ends of what was now unquestionably his own empire of which he was Great King, if he chose to use the title. He did, on some of the coins struck in Asia, though never on his Macedonian ones. Sometimes he was dealing with savage tribes, sometimes with the remains of the Persian army or with feudal lords who didn't know what had hit them. Sometimes there were awkward things, like Greek envoys to the late king to be dealt with. Things had settled down more or less in Greece. Agis from Sparta had attempted an anti-Alexander or anti-League movement, got some sympathy in Athens, but was finally beaten by General Antipater, who sent Spartan hostages off to Alexander. Presumably they had to follow him round in many of his unbelievable wanderings.

There were risings here and there; he usually beat them by surprise attack. Nobody could keep up with his quick decisions and extraordinary marches. But now something happened which was new. His team of young men was beginning to break up through their own pride and jealousy. Some of them were soldiers almost as brilliant as he was; others had gifts as administrators. Many of them, especially the older ones, felt that Alexander should have completed his conquest, taken the treasure and gone back to Macedonia. What did it matter if he left the barbarians in chaos? Philip, his father, had been the Macedonian king chosen by his fighting men, his nobles. But Alexander seemed to have got away from that. They were not his *peers* any longer. Sometimes he seemed even to prefer Persians.

Did he try to talk to the Macedonians about his ideas and failed to get anything across? Perhaps. Parmenion, Philip's general, was one of the least understanding. He had failed at Gaugamela and was in many ways an old nuisance. His advice was not wanted but he always gave it. Philotas his son was in command of the Companions. There was a plot against Alexander's life. Philotas did not report it at once. This was treason.

Philotas was brought to trial before the army, that is, the Macedonian people in arms. The army found him guilty and condemned him to death. Two others implicated in the plot were tried, but found not guilty. Alexander continued them in their commands.

But what about Philotas's father, the old general Parmenion, who would be bitterly angry when the news came to him, who might do anything? Alexander sent a messenger on a racing camel across the desert. Before Parmenion even heard of the death of his son he was assassinated himself. Murder no doubt, but the alternative might have meant the death of many.

Now Alexander was again chasing Bessus, going east up the Helmund valley to the hills. From time to time he founded new Alexandrias, cities which are still there, but have changed over two thousand years. Alexandria of the Arians has become Herat. Alexandria of the Arachosians has become Kandahar. Another Alexandria has become Ghazni. He crossed into the Kabul valley, his troops half blinded by the snow, and here he turned north through the Hindu Kush into Bactria, where

Asian archers, one playing a signal flute: from a vase

Bessus was holding Aornos. Alexander did some amazing crossings of high passes and his troops suffered from cold and hunger. Nobody else has dreamed of taking an army through the highest mountains in the world. It makes Napoleon's crossings of the Alps look very small and easy. But soon the army were to suffer from thirst and heat when they came down into the Oxus plain. Where Bessus had destroyed the boats the soldiers crossed on skins. But the chase was almost over.

Bessus was captured and publicly flogged. Alexander occupied Samarkand, and went on to the very limit of the old Persian empire, leaving garrisons here and there. Then he thought he would hold a grand *durbar* and invite all the leading nobles and *Khans*. But the whole country rose in revolt behind him; his garrisons were killed and the fortresses had to be retaken. He was wounded again. Beyond the boundaries of the Persian empire, across the Jaxartes, mounted men with spears and fur hats jeered at him. He shot at them with catapults, then crossed the river and charged them. Here he got very ill from drinking dirty water and had to be carried to his tent. Alexandria-the-Furthest was founded, the walls quickly built up with sun-dried mud. Today it is called Chodjend.

Now came a war which Alexander nearly lost, with Spitamenes, the Sogdian, a true national war. Alexander's own men were very tired after two years of unrelenting fighting; he left Spitamenes victorious in Bokhara while they rested in winter quarters. It looks as if he, too, was exhausted, as well he might be. Later Bessus came up for judgement; his ears and nose were cut off and he was sent back to Ecbatana for execution.

There was also the gusher of oil that he found by the river Oxus; he sacrificed to avert the evil of this stinking and undrinkable fluid which could suddenly turn into flame. It seems, too, that there was a petroleum well near Ecbatana; but people only thought of it as a natural curiosity. Forty-five posts were built all through Bactria and gradually Spitamenes was worn down. Finally some savage allies killed him and sent his head to Alexander. His daughter Apama was taken prisoner and later on married to one of the most intelligent of the Companions, Seleucus, the commander of the heavy armed infantry, a man who could, incidentally, hold a bull by the horns.

What did someone like Spitamenes look like? Did he wear the kind of clothes one associates with Afghanistan? Was he brown and hook-nosed? We do not even know what gods he worshipped or what language he spoke.

That same summer at Samarkand a terrible thing happened. In the dry heat there was much drinking of local wine. Alexander was not a heavy drinker; he liked talk, and besides he felt, as a pupil of Aristotle must have done, that the important thing was right activity of the mind or soul. The body must be made to obey. He never let himself be deflected by wounds or sickness; perhaps in a way he welcomed them as something to overcome.

But that day he and his friends were all more or less drunk. Cleitus began to tease him; what was at the bottom of it was the dislike of Alexander's Persian appointments and his general good treatment of Persians at the expense of the men, the true breed of Macedonians, who had brought him victory and died for him. Teasing went too far. It looks as though Alexander tried to control himself, but Cleitus stuck his fist under Alexander's nose, saying:

Young man at a feast playing cottabos: tossing wine at a mark

'This saved your life at the Granicus' and went on with the teasing till suddenly Alexander's temper gave way, as Cleitus probably intended, wanting to make him do something he would be ashamed of.

Alexander snatched a spear from a guard. Ptolemy pushed Cleitus out of the hall while some of the others held Alexander down, but he broke away, shouting for Cleitus, who, like the crazy drunk he was for the moment, rushed back and was run through by the spear. A good many of us have seen that kind of quarrel; when it ends as badly as this one did it comes up in the Courts and perhaps someone hangs. But the quarrellers are not men like Cleitus and Alexander.

Alexander came to. He shut himself up for three days in bitter tears, not eating or drinking, calling on his friend Cleitus and sister Lanike, who had been his nurse. Everyone got frightened. What would happen? Alexander's friends persuaded him to eat; the *soothsayers* conveniently explained that Cleitus had incurred the anger of Dionysos for a neglected sacrifice. Many kings have done wrong, but few of them have repented of it so bitterly.

The next winter brought something which Alexander must have enjoyed: the taking of an impregnable fortress. There were still nobles of Sogdiana to be brought into submission. Oxyartes had left his family in a hill fort, the Sogdian rock. Alexander took it with a force of volunteers who climbed the crags with ropes and *pitons* (the first time in history one hears of that method of climbing). One of the prisoners was Oxyartes's daughter, Roxane. Alexander married her, no doubt as a matter of policy and to end the war. They could have had little common language except that of smiles and touches. But let us hope that he loved her at least a little and she him.

53

Into India

It would be quite wrong to think that Alexander was considering anything so definite as conquering the world, although this is how later stories showed him. He had set out to begin with to liberate the Greek cities of Ionia, and to collect some treasure to help his position as overlord of all Hellas. But one thing had led to another. And now he must have seemed to himself to be getting rather nearer to Outer Ocean and the great river imagined by the philosophers so as to tidy up their picture of the world. There was, for that matter, quite a lot of the old Persian empire unconquered. The countries round the Black Sea and Caspian had quietly hived off; often the old kings or rulers were back in command. If Alexander had wanted world conquest it would have been much more natural and sensible to polish off the Mediterranean world first. But that was not what happened.

Meanwhile he had a most complicated civil service and administration to improvise. It would have made things easier if Harpalos had been honest, but Alexander refused to believe that his boyhood friends were behaving as badly as they sometimes did; Harpalos made a fortune for himself on the side. We know that Alexander tried very hard to stop corruption, but plenty of it went on at all levels; he tried also to administer equal justice between people of all races—and was often blamed for it. He had problems of coinage: who was to be allowed to mint

Another piece of gold from the Oxus treasure

the gold and silver and was he to keep Macedonian or
Persian coin values? He did what he could, trying not to
annoy the merchant cities which were used to their own
coinage.

There was no clear distinction between the treasury
and Alexander's own purse, and he was very generous.
For example, he sent back a vast fortune to his old tutor;
one wonders what Aristotle used it for. He was always
founding cities, giving presents or *dowries*, holding
feasts. When the army rested there were always contests,
music or athletics, and the prizes no doubt were provided
by the king.

He gave money generously to the scientists and
historians who were with him, and to Callisthenes, who
probably did him a lot of moral harm, since he flattered

him, wrote about him in a way which would have been bad for anybody, and encouraged him to think of himself as something more than mortal man. Most likely all this was partly in aid of the hopeful restoration of Olynthos, but it does not excuse Callisthenes nor the poets who added their little bit, addressing him as Son of Zeus. This meant nothing to the Persians; they had never thought of their kings as Gods. But the Greeks were hazy about Gods, demi-Gods and semi-divine heroes.

And now Alexander started doing something that was going to make some of his friends very angry. It was bad enough that he should sometimes wear Persian dress, a Persian-type jewelled diadem, and go through Persian court ceremonials, but now he began trying to make people *prostrate* themselves in front of him, go down on their hands and touch their foreheads on to the floor. The Persians didn't mind, because this was how they had always approached the Great King, but the Macedonians were shocked that one civilised man should expect this of another. It meant that their leader and friend, their fellow Macedonian whom they had chosen, was seriously setting up to be a god, which was next thing to a tyrant. And this was not to be borne.

How seriously did Alexander believe this himself? We don't know. Aristotle had told him that when the supreme ruler came he would be as a god among men and Alexander must have felt that by now that was exactly what he was. Perhaps he felt himself only too mortal; he had been wounded, and, worse, laid low with *dysentery*. He wanted to affirm himself against his own body. Or perhaps it was mostly a political idea. Hephaestion supported him but cannot himself ever have thought of Alexander as a god. Anyhow it turned out to be a bad

Down into India: twisting through the Khyber Pass

The north-west frontier of India: these were the kind of mountains which Alexander's armies had to pass

Probably the best copy now existing of the statue of Alexander by Lysippos, his favourite sculptor. This little bronze was made a hundred years or more after the original

One went through the olive groves to Delphi, Apollo's shrine and the centre of Hellas, to consult the oracle

idea, and Callisthenes, who had done so much to bring it about, tried to get out of it. But too late.

One of the royal pages, out hunting, had nipped in front of Alexander and killed the boar himself. By ordinary Macedonian custom he was whipped and had his horse taken away. He and his friends, furious, plotted to kill Alexander. When they were caught they confessed that Callisthenes, who was acting as their tutor in morals and philosophy, had talked to them about the beauty of assassinating tyrants. The pages and Callisthenes were all executed. It was all a great pity, but Callisthenes was only too well avenged by a number of other philosophers, who among them produced a portrait of Alexander as a tyrant, owing everything to luck and other people, and for many years this was believed to be the truth.

But meanwhile Alexander's next step was to stretch his rule over the whole eastern end of the old Persian empire, and this meant thinking about India. The geography he had learned from Aristotle was very vague; he thought of India as a peninsula jutting eastward into the world-encircling river, and crossed by the river Indus. He may have vaguely heard of the river Ganges.

There were older civilisations in India than any in Greece and by now there was a high degree of abstract thought. The idea of 'karma', that what you have done determines what happens to you and what you are, and what you do now makes your future, would have been not unfamiliar to Greek philosophy, though carrying it logically on as the Indians did to *reincarnation*, might have seemed strange to the Greeks. One wishes Alexander could have heard of another king from a kingdom not less prosperous and warlike than Macedon, who had given up all in order to achieve enlightenment, which he

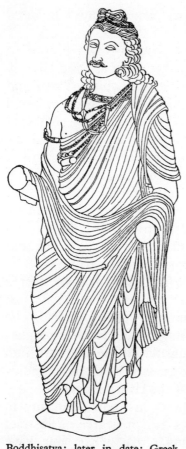
Boddhisatva: later in date: Greek face and drapery: Indian hair and necklaces: a statue

had done in the end and become the Buddha. Siddartha Gautama lived nearly two centuries before Alexander came to India. He is the man whom we know better as the Buddha, the founder of one of the greatest religious and mystical movements of the world. In Indian society there was, and to some extent still is, a division into castes, people with different kinds of interests, thoughts and ways of living, who do not normally mix with one another. The kshatriyas are the warrior caste. Both Siddartha Gautama and the founder of another great Indian religion, the Jains, came from this caste. Had Alexander been an Indian, this would certainly have been his caste too.

The Punjab was reasonably prosperous, based on village communities and village democracy; the actual administration was quite complex, with rules and behaviour laid down. The Persians had exacted some kind of tribute, but were only vaguely overlords. But their dominion had never stretched beyond the Indus river into India itself. Here another young leader and conqueror, Chandragupta, was already building up the foundations of what was to be known to history as the Maurya Empire. This was to stretch right across northern India and become a complete barrier to later attempts at conquest, for instance by Seleucus. We cannot be absolutely sure of dates, but rumours of Chandragupta's armies must certainly have come to Alexander.

We know to some extent how the Greeks took in Indian ways of thought and expression. For instance, the Hindu idea of God usually took shape as Siva and Vishnu. But there was also a cult of Krishna who was God in another form. The Greeks, as always, gave them the names of their own Greek gods, for they too were many-formed and many-named, according to what part of Greece one came from. But what certainly mattered most to Alexander was that the Indians were renowned fighters. He set to work to reorganise his army for the invasion of India, increasing the number of archers, changing some of the commanders and bringing into the Companions some of the sons of Persian nobles. Some of his western soldiers were allowed to go home and he recruited more from the eastern end of what had been the Persian empire.

One thing Alexander was determined on was the exploration of the southern sea. Perhaps the Indian Ocean was really a lake with the farthest part of India joining on to Ethiopia? He talked this over with Nearchus, who always remained his faithful and honest friend, though he for one would never have consented to any nonsense about *prostration*. Nearchus had been appointed a satrap and now was recalled for something much more interesting.

Alexander and his army crossed the Hindu Kush and

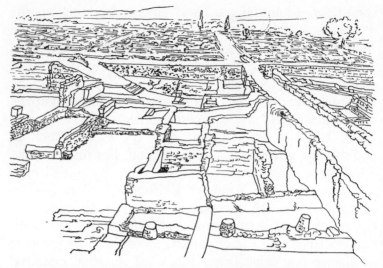
A small part of the remains of the huge, well-planned city of Taxila

came down again on to the Kabul river, where he met the
local khans and also Ambhi, the king of Taxila, capital
of an old civilisation, who is called 'Taxiles' in the
official records. He was at war with a rival king, who is
called 'Porus', because he was king of the Purus or
Pauravas. Alexander would be a most useful ally. 'Taxiles'
gave Alexander twenty-five elephants, but they were
never used in the Macedonian army; the horses would
have had to be trained to get used to them.

Half the army with the baggage was sent down through
the Khyber pass, under Hephaestion and Perdiccas with
'Taxiles'; they must have taken hours and hours to go
through under the grey savage rocks and down the
narrow winding road that never seems to open out.
Meanwhile Alexander himself with the rest of the army
took another route over high passes with hard local
fighting here and there, in the course of which he was

wounded again. This must have been extremely tough going, sometimes involving real mountain climbing. He went down into beautiful flowery Swat (the most delightful country I have ever been in, where Ministers of State still run down mountain goats on foot for the fun of it), where the ivy growing in the mountains made the Macedonians sick for home. Everywhere there was

A sculptured Indian head

tough fighting, and when he came down from Swat into the foothills (a difficult road still) and joined up with Hephaestion, there was more Indian resistance. There seems to have been some large-scale indiscriminate slaughter. One begins to wonder whether impatience to get this phase over, combined no doubt with pain which he may have disregarded, but which was there all the same, was wearing out Alexander's temper, always his weak point.

Hephaestion had thrown a bridge of boats across the Indus above Attock. The armies crossed and no doubt had some rest at Taxila, which must have been a very impressive town, with a university of *Brahmins*, and trading quarters which were beyond anything the Greeks had seen for a long time. And here Alexander and Ambhi of Taxila made their plans for war against 'Porus', the king to the east.

The Ends of the World

The rains were beginning. The king of the Pauravas with all his army was camped on the far bank of the Jhelum. A man could hear the trumpeting of the war elephants and shiver. The *monsoon* clouds were bellying up. While Alexander had a busy-looking force putting out boats opposite 'Porus's' camp, he had the banks *reconnoitred* up and down stream. Eighteen miles above Jhelum, where the river swept round in a great bend, there was a wooded island. An elaborate crossing programme was worked out to take 'Porus' in the flank.

It was a terrible battle, made all the more nightmare-ish by the elephants. The Indian archers had immensely long and powerful bows. The fighting swung up and down in mud and blood, with the monsoon rain blotting out everything but the terrible trumpeting of the elephants. After a harder fight than they had ever yet had, the Macedonians won. The king of the Pauravas was wounded and was surrounded as he lay in the *howdah* of his huge elephant which was carrying him off the battle-field. He was taken to Alexander who asked him how he expected to be treated. 'Like a king,' he answered. And so it was.

But Alexander and the rest never forgot the horror of the elephants, the trampled bodies, the wicked tusks. Years later Seleucus, then a king and married to Apama, daughter of Spitamenes, put a war elephant on to his coinage. The charger Bucephalus had been killed on the battlefield. Alexander named a city after him and Seleucus also put him on a coin.

Head of the Bucephalus from a coin of Seleucus

'Porus' and 'Taxiles' were now reconciled and Alexander decided that he would go to the far end of the old Empire and then sail down the Indus towards outer ocean. He marched east with some difficulty, for the rains were on and the rivers all in flood. He crossed the Ravi, had a desperate battle at Sangala (but so far nobody knows just where this was), where twelve hundred of his men were seriously wounded, and came to the banks of the Beas.

What was on the far side of the Beas? More and larger, and more horrible, elephants. And the army refused to cross. They had finally had enough.

Did Alexander think that if he crossed and fought and won, and perhaps found another river and crossed and fought again, he would come to the very end, to Ocean?

A terrible war elephant

Later writers said so. We don't know. It is very hard to put ourselves anywhere near his state of mind. It is not at all certain that he knew what was building up in front of him. But if the young and victorious Chandragupta had fought the not-now-so-young Alexander with his tired army, it might have been the end of the Macedonians. Alexander waited for three days for the army to say it would, after all, obey him, cross the river and fight. But the Macedonians were as stubborn as their leader. They wanted to go home and by the quickest way. But that was not what they got.

He went back to the Jhelum and finished building his fleet, large and small warships, transport and supply boats. Nearchos the Cretan, the merchant's son, was in command, more honest and faithful than any of the young princes and nobles. He kept a careful and scientific journal from which later geographers learned much. Was he perhaps influenced by Aristotle when he was teaching the boys as a scientist, not as a philosopher or politician? He was the best possible choice. The elephants went by land, and so indeed did much of the army and its Indian allies. But Alexander himself would go with the navy.

He had sacrificed to the great rivers of India, to all his ancestral gods, most of all those whom the Oracle of Ammon had told him to honour, and to Ocean herself. The altars must have been stone-built and high; it is said that Chandragupta sacrificed on them years later. The smoke rose, heavily scented with myrrh and *frankincense* which had been thrown into the flames. Alexander embarked, and standing on the bow of his ship he poured *libations* from a gold cup into the floodwater of the river, to the rivers, to Herakles and Ammon. The

64

trumpets sounded; the oars beat on the water; Alexander was on his way.

He had one more serious campaign against Indians, who cannot quite be identified. One might think that he must have passed the enormous city of Monenjo Daro, though perhaps its golden age was over. But the course of the Indus was probably different, and perhaps the Indian cities he met with are still under the sands of the shifting desert, waiting for the Pakistani

Libation to the gods

archaeologists to find them. What we know is that Alexander took three towns, killing every soul in them in a dreadful slaughter. This may have been because the army was so sick of fighting that they had no time for decency, only longed to be home, and destroyed everything which was in their way. Twice Alexander was first on the ladder up the wall of a besieged citadel, and once shot through the chest by a long arrow. His life was only saved by the holy shield he had taken in Ilium, with which Peucestas, his shield bearer, covered him, while another of his friends, even though he was mortally wounded, kept the attackers off till the army broke in. About July 325 B.C., they were down near the mouth of the Indus; as its course was different it is difficult to identify the place name. Two more Alexandrias were founded—and lost.

At Patala, where the enormous brown Indus divided

into a wild swampy delta with two main channels, Alexander built harbours and docks and did a vast amount of organisation. It must have been the middle of the hot weather and very exhausting. Craterus had already been sent back with the baggage, the elephants, the battered siege towers and rams, and the many sick and wounded. They went up by what is now Quetta, and must have rejoiced in the cooler air and water. India—or that bit of it over which Alexander's armies had marched, and burned and slaughtered—was divided into satrapies, and it was hoped that some taxes at least would come out of it. Craterus probably took back with him gold, jade, jewels and *bronzes* of great beauty.

There was one curious thing. Alexander had given himself time—when?—to meet and talk with some of the wise men, the *gurus*, who, as now in India, had retired from the world and lived in the forest with no possessions, in meditation and discussion. He is said to have set them trick questions which they answered with wisdom. They must have told him how they had escaped from doing, from the Wheel of Things, which drives men through action to desire, to action again, and the destruction and evil that goes with action. Some of them may well have been (as they have been in the past and probably are now) men who had held high position, kings and their ministers, perhaps generals. They talked to him as equals, trying to persuade him of the folly of action, since no man truly owned more than the ground he stood on.

He became fascinated. One day, he may have thought, I too may turn to meditation; I may stop this terrible passion and agitation and action which grips me now. Some of them may have practised versions of the various *yogas* or disciplines over the body, and Alexander, always interested in disciplining the body, would have been impressed. One of them who in the Greek narrative is called 'Calanus', was persuaded to come away with the army and accompanied Alexander on his marches back to Susa.

Then came the exploration of the Indus delta. On the western arm his fleet was caught in the tidal *bore* which swept up the river, terrifying enough for those who had never seen one. Some ships were destroyed, but he sacrificed in due form and sailed out into the Indian Ocean. Here, when he poured his libation, he flung the golden cup into the waves, praying

Another Indian head

that Poseidon, God of all the seas, would bring Nearchos and his fleet safe home. Then he explored the eastern arm, where there was no bore. This seemed the best place to start from.

What Nearchos was to do was entirely practical; he was to establish a practicable trade route between the Indus and the mouth of the Euphrates and so with the western world; he was to sail along the coast noting everything, beaches, harbours, islands, above all, water supplies, to find out if there were any towns or any cultivated land. He was not to look for Outer Ocean or to decide whether he was actually in a land-locked lake or sea, or in fact

67

over the rim of the world. These philosophical questions must wait.

Nearchos would in any case have been bound to keep close in to land, as he could only carry food for ten days and water for five. He took all the larger ships and some smaller ones, probably over a hundred, with some three to five thousand men in them as crews, but also as fighters, since they did not know when or whether they would land among hostile peoples. These ships would be only the size of fishing boats, half-decked or single-decked at best, with simple square sails and with awnings which could be put up for shelter against sun and wind. By now the timing of the monsoon was known, and Nearchos was due to start when the steady north-east wind began to blow. But he sailed earlier, for it looked as though the Indian tribes of the delta were going to attack. The river was still low and he had to cut through the sand bar beyond the mouth and after that was again

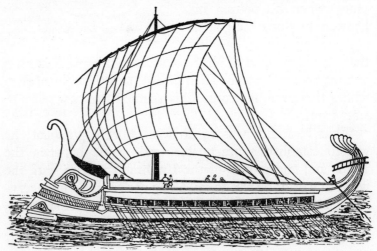

A triseme: a ship with three banks of oars

delayed at what is now Karachi until the hoped-for wind came.

This was the turning point. Alexander must have felt that after this he was going back. In some ways he had failed. He must by this time have realised how vast a world was unconquered and even unexplored. But his last wound had been very severe; the spear may well have punctured a lung. It had left him weakened, even if he refused to admit it.

Yet he was preparing what would turn out to be one of the most famous and difficult marches of his career. If he had known rather more of the geography he might not even have attempted it. But one reason he went was simply that the geography was unknown. Aristotle's pupil had to make it clear for the future, and he took all his surveying section with him as well as the families the soldiers had collected and the traders who followed the army.

His idea was to have a land force supporting the fleet, if necessary digging wells and leaving depots of provisions. He would march along the coast and he hoped to receive the submission of the local people. Up to a point it worked out, but he had not realised the existence of a range of harsh hills rising almost sheer from the coast which forced him to go round the far side into waterless rocky valleys and semi-desert.

Here the guides lost their way. The sand burnt their feet. They ate the baggage mules and camels and burnt the carts for firewood to cook on. If you could not keep up you died. When he saw how it was to be, Alexander, in spite of his wound, sent back his horse to the depot and went on foot with the rest, refusing water when there was not enough to go round. They got back to the sea at last and found fresh water; most of the army were still alive, but many of the others were dead. After this he got to the rock-ringed harbour of Gwadur, and from there found a known route to Pura, where there was one of the old royal palaces where the men could rest and eat. But Alexander was very anxious, for he knew he had failed Nearchos and the fleet. He had not managed to establish the promised wells and food depots. And there was no news of them.

However the fleet had meanwhile been sailing slowly along with a daily stop for food, and, above all, for finding water. Sometimes there was nothing to eat but fish and wild dates and they were down to strict rations. They met with traditional marine wonders: mermaids and monsters. Nearchos ordered them to charge a school of whales in battle order to the sound of war trumpets, and gave thanks to the gods when the whales dived. They found the primitive fish-eaters along the coast, who speared fish with wooden spears or else caught them with palm-fibre nets and ate them raw or dried them in the sun. It was said that they wore only fish skins and lived in huts made of the bones of stranded whales.

But at last, after nearly three months voyage, Nearchos sighted the hills of the Arabian coast at the entrance to the Persian Gulf. The fleet sailed through the Straits of Ormuz and anchored in the Amasis river. They had only lost four ships. Nearchos managed to find his way to Alexander, who by now had halted his march at Gulash-kird. How they must have talked, and how happy they must have been to see one another again! It was wonderful for Alexander to have someone he could trust so completely. There was a short break ahead of them, a time of real rejoicing, for Craterus had joined them with his

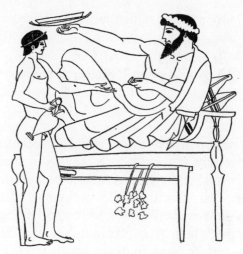
Another feast scene from a vase

army, which had crossed by Kandahar and the regular caravan route across the Lut desert. Now they held traditional games and feasts; another Alexandria was founded. It is from here that the story comes of the drunken procession reeling through Carmania with Alexander at the head on a great wheeled float, dressed as the God Dionysos. Perhaps some of them did get drunk; but they deserved a holiday and a way of forgetting after all they had gone through.

71

The Great Loving Cup

Alexander was twenty-seven. He had been away too long. He brought his army to Susa in the spring, while Nearchos brought the fleet round through the Persian Gulf. Here he found endless reports, letters and messengers or envoys waiting for him. His empire was in a miserable state of confusion. Some of the satraps had behaved well, sent in their taxes and ruled justly, but others had set themselves up as independent rulers, kept the money, hired mercenaries and murdered their subjects. There were pretenders to the Persian throne, perhaps of the royal blood, springing up, each with his little army of followers. The tomb of Cyrus had been broken into and plundered of gold and jewels; so had several temples. There had been a famous royal stud of horses; two-thirds had been stolen. His own Macedonians had joined in all this. Cleomenes who had been left in charge in Egypt was one of the offenders. Worst and sorest, his boyhood friend Harpalos, whom he had trusted in spite of warnings, had made a fortune out of the civil service in tax collection and had behaved outrageously. When he heard that Alexander was after all coming back, he fled into Greece. Here he was killed later by one of his own accomplices.

It had all happened because they thought Alexander had disappeared for ever. On the face of it you would think it almost impossible to survive all those wounds and sicknesses, the cold and the heat, the marches that become more incredible the more one knows the country. Some of them must have prayed for his death many times and it must often have been rumoured. But after all he had survived. He was on to them like a lion.

The thing that strikes one is that Alexander really hated oppression, even of the most ordinary of his subjects, even of women. He was Greek enough really to believe in freedom. He struck hard. He had four Persian satraps seized, tried and executed. He also executed three generals, one of whom was a Macedonian noble. Two of the pretenders were captured. Cyrus's tomb was restored; so no doubt were the temples. All satraps had to disband their mercenaries. There were now satrapies needing to be filled and these had to be given to loyal Macedonians.

As four of the chief Persians had been executed, it was essential to reassure the Persian people. One of the few men who was prepared to take the trouble to do this was Peucestas, who had saved Alexander's life by holding the sacred shield of Ilium over him at that terrible Indian battle; he had been Alexander's shield bearer for a long time now and that probably meant being with him a great deal and hearing him talk. He understood many of Alexander's ideas, took the trouble to learn Persian, wore Persian clothes and helped a great deal to quiet the feelings of the Persians when he was made satrap of Persis and Susiana. We can picture Alexander always talking to the men round him, whoever they were, trying out ideas, questioning and making them answer. Aristotle must have taught him that this was the right way to go about it. And on some of them the ideas took.

It was at Susa that the Indian guru felt death coming

on him. He asked for a funeral *pyre* to be built. Alexander did not want to do this, but 'Calanus' persuaded him that it was for the best, mounted the pyre, and willed himself into death. As his body burned the trumpets sounded and the elephants, throwing back their trunks, gave a royal salute. Before mounting the pyre he had said farewell to the generals but not to Alexander. To him he only said: 'We shall meet again in Babylon.'

It had now become an essential part of Alexander's ideas not merely to reconcile Persians to Macedonians, but to *fuse* east and west in a state of 'homonoia', of brotherhood and friendship. And by now he must have thought beyond the Persian civilisation and language to all the Asian countries, all the languages and customs and gods which he had seen and honoured, trying to understand them, becoming aware of the culture, both material and spiritual, that never belongs to one nation or group alone, but is shared by all. How could he achieve this mixing and sharing? He must at least make one grand effort. This he did at Susa, when he planned an enormous wedding feast, which was to be a true mixing in one great loving cup. He and Hephaestion, still and always his dearest friend, were to marry Darius's two daughters, the little princesses, Barsine and Drypetis; they were probably still only children. He himself was already married to Roxane the Sogdian, so that now he would be entwined, like the ivy of Dionysus, with two very different parts of the eastern world.

He encouraged his army to marriage. Eighty of his officers married noble girls from the Persian or near-Persian great families. Many of the soldiers in his armies had found themselves native 'wives' during their wanderings, and many had brought them with them.

74

Another golden object from the Oxus treasure

Now they were to be married by the most solemn and sacred rites. Here there would surely be much mingling of Indian blood. The marriages could probably go only one way, as there would be hardly any Greek or Macedonian girls so far from home. The sad thing was that later on some of these officers sent away their Persian or Asiatic wives, whom they had only married to please Alexander. But Seleucus and Apama were the founders of a great *dynasty*.

At the same time Alexander undertook to pay the army's debts and invited all the debtors to put down their names on a roll. This was done partly because Alexander sensed bad feeling growing up among his men. It was partly due to all they had been through and their longing to go home. It was also because the armies were to be increased by an enrolment of thirty thousand young men, Persians or Asians of some kind, who had been trained in the same way as Macedonians. Were these,

Alexander, from a coin

the army felt, to be the new favourites of their king and leader? Even in the exclusive cavalry there were more and more non-Macedonians. And there was all this wearing of Persian dress by somebody who should have considered himself exclusively the leader of the Macedonians! So the talk went. Some of the men had a feeling that this paying of their debts was only a trick to discover which of them was spending money beyond his pay. When Alexander found that this was the feeling he paid everybody in cash without even asking their names.

Meanwhile Alexander felt that there was work of conciliation to do in Greece itself. He sent a decree to be read out by the heralds in the sacred and peaceful atmosphere of the Olympic Games, asking the mainland city states of the League of Corinth to take back their exiles with their families. The exiles, who had heard about the decree and who were there at the Games, were of course deeply enthusiastic. This was one of Alexander's exciting and risky ideas, because among the exiles who would go back to the city states were many of his enemies or those whom Antipater, his general, had charged with being his enemies. It would also help to keep the peace of the world if this great floating body of homeless men could go home; it would mean there were fewer mercenaries for any future rebel leaders to use.

Antipater was getting to be an old man now with an able and ambitious son, Cassander. He was always complaining to Alexander about his mother, and no doubt Queen Olympias was a difficult person to get on with and apt to interfere with policy. But what Alexander

76

said was that Antipater could never manage to understand that one tear from Olympias would outweigh all his complaints. Now he thought things would work out better if Antipater was recalled and Craterus took his place.

But this admirable decree about the exiles was accompanied by something which was not so wise. Yet logically perhaps it had to come, since the decree broke the covenant of the League of Corinth which forbade interference with internal affairs by Alexander. So it seemed that the best way out of it would be if the cities would, like the empire, accept him as a god. He asked that all the cities in the League would take steps to make him a god. Most of them took this as a *whim* and proceeded to go through the ceremonials of *deification*. But Athens opposed it at first and only agreed with the rest of the city states when she found that Alexander was really in earnest and that it was risky to oppose him. So he became a god in Athens too. One wonders what Aristotle, now an old man—he died two years later— must have thought of his pupil. He would have disapproved profoundly, and yet it was partly his own doing.

In any case the whole thing was purely formal. No educated Greek believed in the gods in any real sense; to put a mortal commander-in-chief among them was only to make them look still more unreal. Nor can one suppose that Alexander himself took it seriously—or did he sometimes just for a moment? Was it partly to check that tendency in himself that he had liked talking with his Indian guru, for whom the idea of God was so totally different that the notion of a deified soldier was merely ridiculous? Siddartha Gautama had ended not as a god but as a Buddha, one who has attained wisdom, the way out, the ultimate gateway of enlightenment. And that is always attainable, though so few ever get there.

Antipater however was deeply shocked, as were a few old-fashioned people. Queen Olympias perhaps felt that this was something she had known all along. It may have worried some of the senior Macedonians in the army. Yet it was not what brought about the real trouble in the army.

What was so desperately upsetting to officers and men alike was the feeling that their Alexander was turning them out from their place next to his heart and replacing them with a lot of dirty foreigners, for so the old stiffs who had fought at Granicus and Issus and at Gaugamela must have thought of the Persians; they would remind one another of Persian treachery and beastliness, of the sick men slaughtered in their beds at Issus and this and that. And here was Alexander marrying one of them, making the Persians into his kinsmen! Everything was wrong: wearing Persian dress, trying to make them do this stupid Persian prostration, preferring Persians to them!

All this, coupled with their misery in never getting home, not knowing if their wives and families were alive or dead, was too much for them. Alexander proposed to send home all veterans who were past service, with Craterus when he went back to the west, taking over from Antipater. The Macedonians got into their heads that this meant that Alexander himself never intended to go home. He meant to stop being a Macedonian, instead to become altogether a Persian and govern from Susa or Babylon. This was all wrong. Alexander never meant anything of the sort. He meant to go home—soon— as soon as everything was tidied up—and see his mother again. But the army had got to the point where they could no longer see reason. At Opis all of them except the guards who were closest to him broke into mutiny, threatening and shouting at him.

This was not the way to get what you wanted out of Alexander. It only sent his temper flying. The guards arrested the ringleaders for mutiny and he himself made a passionate speech to the troops. 'Now, as you all want to go,' he shouted, 'Go, every one of you and tell them at home that you deserted your king who had led you from victory to victory across the world, and left him to the care of the strangers he had conquered! And no doubt your word will win you the praises of men and the blessing of heaven. Go!'

Perhaps he made this speech from the balcony of the palace, just above the heads of the crowd of soldiers waving their swords and pikes at him. Then he turned fiercely away, he turned his back on them and burst through his friends into his own room. Here, as after Cleitus's murder, he shut himself up and would not speak or eat. No doubt this got through to the army.

When he felt able, when the burning of anger was over, he called on the Persian leaders and asked them to start the formation of a Persian army. But the regiments were still to carry the old Macedonian names. And it was this that broke the will and anger of the army. They came running and stumbling, gathering in knots and finally in a great crowd in front of the palace, calling on him by name, refusing to be moved off.

He came out and he could not speak. There were tears running down his face. One of them began haltingly to say: 'You have made Persians into your kinsmen' but Alexander broke in, and they must all have gone dead quiet to hear. 'But I make you all my kinsmen!'

And then the army, the thousands and thousands of Macedonians, burst into wild cheering. He came down to them and all who would kissed him. The anger was over. All was forgiven on both sides.

The veterans—ten thousand of them—were still to go home with Craterus, but before they left there was something more to be done. Alexander decided to have a great feast, to which all should be invited, a party for everyone, at which all should be equally welcome. At his own table were Macedonians and Persians, the enemies reconciled, and men from every other race in his empire as well as Greeks, who were of his world but not under his direct rule. When the feast ended there came the solemn libations, the offering of wine to the watching

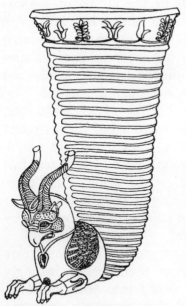

A great silver and gilt Persian drinking-horn

gods. At Alexander's table the wine was poured from the enormous silver loving cup which had once belonged to Darius, but now was to belong to the world. A trumpet sounded and all those thousands at the feast made libation together, led by the Persian Magi, followers of Zoroaster, and the Greek priests or seers.

After the libation came Alexander's prayer. All that we know of it are a few words, a summary which was made by someone who had only heard of it, or perhaps felt cynical about it, certain as most people are that human nature cannot change. Yet perhaps they were wrong, and so are all of us who say that you can never trust anyone and that there will always be wars. And perhaps after all Alexander was right. For he prayed for peace. He prayed that Macedonians and Persians and all the people of his empire might be partners alike and that the peoples of the world he knew might live together in *harmony* and in unity of heart and mind. This was the true 'homonoia'. He said, in words of which we cannot be certain, that all men are sons of one father. And he believed himself that he had been sent to be, not the conqueror, but the *reconciler* of mankind.

More gold from the Oxus treasure

The End

What are we to make of this? Was this perhaps the great secret which the Oracle of Ammon told him? Or is it just that in their hearts mankind have always wanted peace and brotherhood, the garden of Eden, and most of all in times of violence and uncertainty, pain and death, and that we have laid our wish on to our heroes? Could Alexander have seen as clearly as this, and if so how did the message become twisted and falsified so soon after his time? Was it simply because nobody else really understood? Men are blinded by jealousies and arrogance and ambition. They cannot see far enough. They are too small. Only the great can afford to say the things which seem to be so obviously impossible to the smaller ones, but they are not believed. Or not until long after their time, when the rest of the world haltingly begins to catch up, as we begin to catch up with the prayer of Alexander.

The guests left the feast quietly, most of them with more to think about than they could manage. Perhaps some did not understand at all. A few here and there were fired. Hephaestion understood. But there was a terrible thing yet waiting for Alexander. That autumn at Ecbatana, Hephaestion died. He was next to Alexander, not only as the one most loved, but as the highest in rank. He was in command of all who remained of the original Companions who set out from Macedonia, and in Persian terms he was the *Grand Vizier*.

Alexander in bitter misery ordered a royal pyre to be built and commanded that his friend be honoured for ever as a hero, that is, a demi-god. Then he went away into the hills of Luristan to fight and subdue the hill tribes there and try to forget his pain. In spring he came back to Babylon. He had plenty on hand. Envoys came to him from Italy and this might have been the beginning of a move towards the western end of the Mediterranean if things had turned out otherwise. But the main interest was in exploration, and the man he must have talked with most was Nearchos.

He had to decide whether the Caspian Sea was a lake or part of an ocean of some sort. He sent an exploring party north to find out. But the Persian Gulf was more important. The Tigris must be made completely *navigable*; yet another Alexandria was founded at the mouth. At Babylon he began to build a great harbour for the merchant ships that were to come from all over the world. The eastern coast of the Persian Gulf was to be colonised; he sent gold to be coined at Sidon and used to buy or hire sailors and colonists. But his fleet must also sail clear round Arabia, which would open a trade route to Egypt and further advance exploration.

He began to get some larger ships built in Phoenicia and hauled overland in sections to Thapsacus and from there floated down the Euphrates. Nobody knew quite how big Arabia really was. He sent the ships south which came to the incense land of the Yemen. Others discovered the island of Bahrein. Alexander himself would sail with the great fleet and there would be Nearchos to talk to, even if he could never be so loved as Hephaestion had been.

But meanwhile he must look himself at the irrigation

canals and the cuts which took off the flood water from the great rivers, especially those which had been broken down during the war with Xerxes and never properly rebuilt. Perhaps he slapped his hand at a biting mosquito, but paid little attention to so small an enemy. Envoys with petitions had come over from Greece; they came to see him, garlanded as to a temple.

But that biting mosquito had brought him the deadly disease of *malaria*. As the fever came back again and again he grew weaker. He thought he would recover; he talked constantly to Nearchos about their plans. But the time came when he was too ill for speech; even he must have known that the end was coming, as it had come for Hephaestion. He was carried into the great palace, and here the army, in terrible distress, insisted on seeing him. They filed through the room where he lay dying, just able to move his head in farewell. That night some of the generals enquired of some Babylonian god, perhaps the Babylonian Herakles, if Alexander should be brought into his temple. The oracle replied that it would be best for him where he was. Two days later he died, on the 13th of June 323. Perhaps that was the best. To carry back bright to the coiner the mintage of man—the man Alexander of Macedon who had prayed for peace, and at last himself received it.

Afterwards

The next twenty years were a terrible struggle between the Generals and princes and others who came and went, for Alexander's Empire, or bits of it. Because of this, thousands of people, right across the middle of the known world, were killed or had their homes and harvests burnt. The would-be rulers were utterly merciless to one another. Some like Eumenes were loyal to the house of Alexander and his son by Roxane, not even born when his father died; others saw that the Empire was bound to break up, and, like Ptolemy with Egypt, put all their strength and cunning into getting the bit they wanted. Nearchos was not one of the ambitious ones; perhaps in the end he retired to a great estate in his native Crete, or perhaps he set out to explore some far coast and never came back. For twenty years the world was full of murder and torture and occasional heroism; there were terrible scenes, as when the Macedonian soldiers refused to kill Queen Olympias, at last, after bitter fighting, in the power of her enemies; only the kinsfolk of those she had murdered were ready to drive home the knife.

By the end of the fourth century the situation became calmer; the new kings had begun to strike their own coins instead of using Alexander's head. Seleucus and Apama reigned in the east; Ptolemy had Egypt; Antipater's son, Cassander, was king of Macedon. But Syria, Phrygia and Caria were still being passed about and struggled for.

Antigonos, who had ruled justly, if sometimes harshly, had just been killed, but his able son, Demetrios, was still in command of an army, and due to make a come-back. These wars always cost money, and taxes weighed heavily on peasant and merchant alike.

But the most important thing which had happened was that the world had opened out, in the way it did later on after the discovery of America. Intelligent people could never any longer think of themselves simply as citizens of their own little State or city. An Athenian could no longer feel that Athens had a right to consider herself the leader of civilisation. Instead of breaking up increasingly into separate dialects, Greek came to be the 'koine', the common speech in which, for instance, the New Testament is written.

India now knew about Europe, just as Europe did about India; old stories could be checked against facts. Artistic influence went both ways. If you look at the sculptures which were made round and beyond the north-west frontiers of India, it is very difficult to know if they are Greek or Indian. Thousands of horses are said to be descended from Bucephalus, thousands of men and women from Alexander. The people of Kafristan, who make extraordinary wooden statues of men on horses, supposed themselves to be descended from Macedonian soldiers. If you speak of Alexander today in Swat it is as though you spoke of a familiar figure who passed only lately across the high passes and through the apricot orchards by the river.

There was, of course, no colour bar in the days we have been thinking about. This is a most un-natural thing, only recently invented in the interests of a few stupid and frightened people. One part of Alexander's policy was always taken up by his successors. They all founded cities, some of which survived. Each city meant a mixing of races.

Yet it was not only the east that claimed Alexander. Perhaps even in his lifetime the story tellers of all countries were busy spinning their tales about him. After he died a huge web of stories grew up, some based on a half truth, others completely imaginary. They come in twenty-four different languages, and each language and group makes him their special hero. In the Jewish story, for instance, he becomes the master of the magic Throne of Solomon, who shuts up the giants Gog and Magog behind iron gates. For them, and also for the Islamic world, he was Alexander the two-horned, since his coins show him with the ram's horns, symbols of the god Ammon. The Bedouin recognised him in Napoleon. But the Abyssinians thought of him as a saint. In the Persian story he goes beyond India, always conquering, crosses Tibet, China and Russia till at last he reaches the Land of Darkness. But the Babylonians say he came to the Well of the World's End and drank the waters of life. Never is he a dead man, but rather an ever-living hero.

So it goes on. There is something about the story of Alexander that grips everyone. In the old days this meant making up more chapters to the story. Today it means that the historians come under the spell. Look at Volume VI of the CAMBRIDGE ANCIENT HISTORY. Some of the chapters are a bit stodgy. But when Tarn starts writing about Alexander, the whole thing flares up into something we read eagerly. Tarn added his garland to those of the ancient worshippers in the Temple who looked on Alexander as a son of God. I too throw my handful of incense on the smouldering altar flame.

How Do We Know?

Very little has survived of the first sources, which, if only they were complete, would give us a clear story. There are only fragments of the official Journal by Eumenes and his staff, and an occasional sentence from the reports by a few of the surveyors. There are a few inscriptions of the time, decrees and temple lists, showing, for example, who gave things or dedicated statues. A good deal of Isocrates is left, and several of the Orations of Demosthenes which tell us something of the earlier part of the story, in particular, and of course the books of Aristotle, especially the *Ethics* and *Politics*. Some of the other orators speak of Philip or Alexander; one must pick up whatever is going.

The histories written at the time only survive in an occasional sentence or passage quoted by someone else. This goes for Nearchos and Ptolemy, as well as for Callisthenes, and Polyclitos who was essentially a geographer.

But later on there are solid bits of history, including, of course, Plutarch's *Life of Alexander*. Plutarch was one of the writers who fell under the Alexander spell, and when he wanted to emphasise a point, he would make up a story or quote one which was certainly invented long after the event. He quoted conversations and letters; they make the history of Alexander much more vivid and interesting, but they just cannot be accepted as being true. However, all this makes Plutarch good reading.

The other main historians are Arrian, Diodorus and Q. Curtius Rufus. There are odd bits here and there in various later historians, Strabo, Aelian, Pausanias, and others. One has, if possible, to check all this up against what is known for certain.

But books are not everything. There are the remains of the various cities which Alexander fought over or founded or restored. People in Alexandria today are still hoping to discover Alexander's tomb, and if one finds the tram lines all up and great holes in a main street, it may mean that they are on the track at last. We can date the rebuilding of the temple of E-sagila in Babylon. Taxila has been splendidly excavated, and there is a fascinating museum on the edge of the cliffs above the river. More Alexander material is quite likely to be found in Pakistan, especially if the old course of the Indus can be reconstructed. There are exhibits in the museum at Peshawar which give one a vivid idea of the east-west current of ideas. But the Victoria and Albert Museum, and also the British Museum, have some interesting sculpture and objects of the period or a little later, some of which are illustrated in this book.

By now we know a good deal about earlier climates. We cannot be absolutely certain that it was malaria which killed Alexander, but it seems, from the accounts, to be very probable indeed.

A certain amount of armour, contemporary weapons, etc. remains, and so, of course, do various buildings or the ruins of them. There are bronze and gold objects, jewellery, enough coins to help us over what some of the famous people looked like, and there are copies of Lyssippus's portrait statues of Alexander. We have plenty of evidence on what Egypt was like at this time, both from papyrus letters, lists, orders, and so on, and from all kinds of objects, including cloth, which have survived in the dry sands of Egypt.

Quantities of historians have written about Alexander, in most languages. Something fresh may turn up any day, or a new interpretation may be put on to known facts, and if this is interesting and likely to add to our knowledge, a paper will probably come out in some learned journal, in almost any part of the world.

Things to Do

1. Look at the silver coins of Philip, Alexander, and the Generals who succeeded him. Some of them kept on putting Alexander's head on to their coins, so that people would think they were his true heirs. Most big museums have some.

2. Find out how high Alexander went when he took his armies across the Hindu Kush. Who else has climbed there? Could he see Everest?

3. Look at Egyptian things of this period in the British Museum. Which do you think Alexander might have seen? There are some in other big museums as well.

4. Look up what is said about Tyre, Sidon and Babylon in the Old Testament. Why do you think the Israelites disliked them so much?

5. Show, with maps, what difference it would have made to Alexander if he had been able to use a railway, a telephone or a troop ship.

6. Imagine you are a surveyor with the Macedonian army: send an account of your last week's work to the official records department under Eumenes.

7. If you live near London, go and see the things from Bactria and thereabouts in the Victoria and Albert Museum.

8. If you live in Pakistan, visit the excavations and museum at Taxila, and look at the Bactrian and Kafristan things in the museum at Peshawar.

9. Find out, and write down, what are the modern names of the places on the map (when they are different from the ones you see). Find out and write down what countries they are in now.

10. Suggestions for pictures to draw:—

(a) Alexander taming Bucephalus.
(b) Alexander feasting in King Darius's tent.
(c) Alexander sailing down the Nile.
(d) Alexander marching over the Hindu Kush.

11. Write a dialogue between two Macedonians in Alexander's army, one of whom admires him while the other criticises him.

12. Write a letter from one of Alexander's soldiers home to his wife, telling her about the army's adventures.

13. Discuss in class Alexander's ideal of world brotherhood. Did he try to get this in the right kind of way? How are we trying to get it today?

14. If Alexander had lived today he would probably not have died of malaria. Find out about the methods by which we fight malaria successfully today. How were they discovered?

15. If you have a pony, take him to see an elephant and see what happens. Or, if you have an elephant, take him to see a pony.

Glossary

The meanings given here explain how the words are used in this book; you may find other meanings in a dictionary.

archaeologist: someone who finds out about early men by digging up their houses, graves, etc.
attar of roses: special perfume made from roses
barbarians: people other than Greeks
bore: strong tide rushing up narrow river-mouth
Brahmin: Indian belonging to the highest, learned caste or group
breach: break or gap in a wall
bronzes: statues made of bronze, a mixture of copper and tin
colonnade: series of columns linked by arches
deification: making a man into a god
delta: mouth of a river which spreads out into a triangle of little streams and swamps
democracy: government by all the people
dowry: money or property owned by a girl at marriage
durbar: grand review attended by princes with all their followers
dynasty: family of rulers
dysentery: disease usually caught in hot, dirty places
envoy: messenger
to equate: to make equal or to match
ethics: study of right and wrong behaviour of people
fertility: richness of land in growing crops.
frankincense: kind of gum sweet-smelling when burnt
frieze: coarse cloth like canvas
to fuse: to join together so that one melts into the other
Grand Vizier: kind of Prime Minister
guru: Indian wise man
harmony: being in tune with one another
Hellas: Greece
Hellenes: Greeks
howdah: seat, with awning and curtains, placed on an elephant
impregnable: impossible to capture
indiscriminate: treating everyone alike
irrigation: system of streams dug by men to water dry land
javelin: small spear thrown by hand
Khan: title given to a ruler in Asia

libation: a pouring out of wine to the gods
liberation: act of gaining freedom
liberator: someone who gives people freedom
malaria: fever caught from mosquito bites
mercenary: soldier who fights for pay rather than for his country
metaphysics: study of the meaning of life and of the world
mole: stone causeway built out into water
monsoon: very heavy rains at one particular time of year in Asia
myrrh: bitter-smelling gum
navigable: water on which boats can be sailed
oligarchy: government by few rich men
oracle: voice foretelling the future, thought to be a god speaking through
    a priest
orator: great public speaker
to outflank: to march round and attack from the side
papyrus: paper made from tall grass growing by the Nile in Egypt
parchment: writing material made from animal skins
peer: equal
phalanx: soldiers grouped closely together with shields touching
piton: spike used in climbing mountains
to prostrate oneself: to bow down to the ground
prostration: act of bending to the ground
pyre: pile of wood on which a human body was burnt.
ram: long, heavy weapon swung by team of soldiers to knock down walls
to reconcile: to make people friends again
to reconnoitre: to spy out the land
refurbished: old but brought up-to-date
reincarnation: belief that the spirits of men, when they die, are re-born
    in new bodies
rites: solemn ceremonies
sarissa: long-handled spear
satrap: governor of a province in Persia
scythed chariot: small horse car with long knives on it, driven into battle
serf: slave
siege tower: movable tower used to besiege castles or cities
soothsayer: fortune-teller
tribute: money paid by conquered people to the conqueror
whim: mere fancy
withies: stems of bushes used instead of ropes
yoga: Hindu discipline of body and soul, aimed at attaining union with
    God